ANTIRACISM

D0104304

Antiracism

An Introduction

Alex Zamalin

NEW YORK UNIVERSITY PRESS
New York

NEW YORK UNIVERSITY PRESS
New York
www.nyupress.org

References to Internet websites (URLs) were accurate at the time of writing. Neither the author nor New York University Press is responsible for URLs that may have expired or changed since the manuscript was prepared.

Library of Congress Cataloging-in-Publication Data
Names: Zamalin, Alex, 1986–   author.
Title: Antiracism : an introduction / Alex Zamalin.
Description: New York : New York University Press, [2019] |
Includes bibliographical references and index.
Identifiers: LCCN 2018026985| ISBN 9781479849284 (cl : alk. paper) |
ISBN 9781479822638 (pb : alk. paper)
Subjects: LCSH: Anti-racism—United States. | United States—Race relations.
Classification: LCC E184.A1 Z36 2019 | DDC 305.800973—dc23
LC record available at https://lccn.loc.gov/2018026985

New York University Press books are printed on acid-free paper, and their binding materials are chosen for strength and durability. We strive to use environmentally responsible suppliers and materials to the greatest extent possible in publishing our books.

Manufactured in the United States of America

10 9 8 7 6 5 4 3 2 1

Also available as an ebook

For Alison, Sam, and Anita

CONTENTS

1

The Origins of American Antiracism

August 11, 2017, shocked many Americans. Hundreds of white supremacists gathered in the university town of Charlottesville, Virginia, screaming, "Jews will not replace us!" and the Nazi slogan "Blood and Soil!" under the banner of "Unite the Right." What were once Klan hoods were replaced with khakis and polo shirts. Nazi swastikas were abandoned in favor of Confederate flags. But the message was clear to anyone who paid attention. These white nationalists felt emboldened to go public, especially after the shock of 2016: the election of the Republican president Donald Trump, who ran a campaign dubbed "Make America Great Again!," which played on the fantasy that certain parts of America had been taken away, besmirched, denigrated, and abused after eight years of the first black president, Barack Obama. Trump's campaign embraced the racist far right, the so-called alt-right, which calls for reclaiming European American civilization and warns of a "white genocide," a supposed conspiracy that lax immigration standards, combined with progressive social welfare initiatives, are secretly designed to eliminate the white American majority and make America into a majority-minority nation. What was even more disturbing for many people, however, was that just a week after the Charlottesville rally, which concluded with one of the white supremacists driving over and killing a nonviolent white protestor, Trump delivered a press conference in which he equated white supremacists with the counterprotestors. Both sides were wrong and had bad people, he said. As he put it, "And you had, you had a group on one side that was bad. And you had a group on the other side that was also very violent. And nobody wants to say that, but I'll say it right now. You had a group—you had a group on the other side that comes charging in without a permit, and they were very, very violent."[1]

Charlottesville was a reminder that racism has always been indigenous to US history. But it also revealed racism's greatest existential threat. Charlottesville counterprotestors were part of a long US tradition of citizens who were not shocked by but expected racism. These citizens countered racist ideas, attacked racial inequality, and threatened racism's grip on power. They constitute the antiracist American political tradition on which American democracy's future depends. *Antiracism* tells their story.

Racism and Antiracism

In order for racism to make sense, it has been based in a philosophy of hierarchy, identity, and difference. Before the seventeenth century, it was justified theologically and biblically. A passage from the book of Genesis, which describes the "Curse of Ham"—whose descendents were condemned to bondage for his mistreatment of his father, Noah—was used to justify the subjugation of people with darker skin. But soon this theological explanation morphed into something more scientific.

From the moment the word appeared in a Spanish dictionary in 1611, as *raza*, a kind of authentic, well-bred horse, race has been associated with subhuman characteristics. The modern idea of racism was born out of the eighteenth-century wish to scientifically categorize humanity's essential hereditary traits—what was known as racial identity. Among the most important figures in this regard was the Swedish naturalist Carl Linnaeus, who in 1735 tried to categorize the various races—Europeans, Asians, Indians, Africans. Europeans had traits associated with upstanding citizenship, deference to the law, and rationality, while Africans were perceived as lazy and fickle. Johann Friedrich Blumenbach, for his part, did not impute normative value to race in the same way as Linnaeus and, unlike him, believed all humanity descended from a common source. But his *On the Natural Varieties of Mankind* (1775) nonetheless connected white people to the "Caucasus" and depicted them as the most beautiful and aesthetically pleasing.[2]

Despite these naturalist arguments' claim to scientific objectivity and value neutrality, they became the perfect way to endow moral value to skin color and, therefore, to justify the enslavement and economic, political, and cultural exploitation of nonwhite people throughout the globe. Although racism contradicted the Enlightenment idea that all people are born equal with inalienable rights such as freedom and human dignity, it became a total ecosystem that created obscene differences in people's life chances. White people got political rights and physical safety. What nonwhite people got instead was something brutal: enslavement of their bodies, imperialist exploitation of their natural resources, and dehumanization of their spirit.[3]

But racism did not go unopposed in the US; it created the antiracist. The first antiracists, antislavery abolitionists from the American founding in the late eighteenth century until emancipation after the end of the Civil War in 1865, struggled against the systematic exploitation of black labor under slavery. The next major wave came after the end of the Reconstruction period (1865–1877) and during the Jim Crow era in the 1890s through the civil rights movement of the 1950s and 1960s, when antiracists challenged the destruction of black bodies under lynching and the dehumanizing second-class citizenship of "separate but equal" public facilities that was formalized by the infamous Supreme Court decision *Plessy v. Ferguson* (1896). Ever since the 1960s, in what has been described as the "post-civil-rights era," antiracists have challenged de facto segregation, a condition in which racial equality is formalized within antidiscrimination law. But a long history of racial inequality and its aftereffects has led to the clustering of black citizens in eviscerated segregated neighborhoods and disparities in income, wealth, education, mass incarceration, and rates of police brutality.

Throughout history, antiracists have engaged in various strategies of resistance, some of which were successful and others of which were not. They have championed the idea of liberation but sometimes have been blind to their own exclusionary commitments when it came to gender, class, sexuality, and even race. But their overarching focus has been on challenging racism. Many of their counterarguments and direct actions assaulted racism's public face, its most visible enforcer: the unmistakable American racist—the slaveholder, lyncher, Ku Klux Klansman, social Darwinist, eugenicist, southern Democrat, and neo-Nazi. But antiracists have also, and perhaps even more importantly, unmasked racism's secret weapon: the ordinary white American who has sometimes tepidly, conditionally, equivocally, or even shamefully agreed with the unmistakable racist.

Some antiracists have called out racists' bad faith and malicious fantasy of a white utopia in segregated, enclosed communities free from the burden of black thoughts. Some have rejected as dubious the demands for empirical evidence before believing that the first black US president, Barack Obama, is truly an American citizen, rather than an anticolonial radical Kenyan. Others have debunked the myth that single black mothers, so-called welfare queens, exploit Social Security and Medicaid benefits. Some have rendered absurd the idea that black culture has no interest in educating its youth. And still others have attacked the instruments used to secure racial inequality: voting-booth intimidation, the separation of powers, checks and balances, murder, rape, terrorism, sterilization, redlining, redistricting, jails, prisons, and the police.[4]

Antiracist Thought and Politics in History

Antiracism has had an extensive intellectual and political history in the US. Colloquially, the term *antiracist* captures a wide range of meaning—from those who simply claim that they are not racist or oppose racism to those who see it as an injustice inconsistent with American values or try to excise it from their lives and society. From this understanding, almost every American today might call themselves antiracist. Since the gains of the civil rights movement, the end of Jim Crow, and the election of Barack Obama in 2008 and 2012, antiracism has become a public kind of aspiration, even if only in word and rhetoric. This idea stems from the belief that Americans live (or should aspire to live) in a "color-blind" society, that is, a society in which skin color or racial identity no longer matters. Consequently, antiracism has become both ubiquitous and often defanged of its critical and transformative social potential.

For instance, Black Lives Matter activists struggling against police brutality claim the title. But so too do major American corporations through their diversity-training initiatives and hiring of nonwhite CEOs. Educators call for developing an antiracist education by challenging dominant narratives of American progress. Yet opponents of racial equality use Martin Luther King Jr.'s argument that citizens should judge people by the content of their character rather than the color of their skin to argue against affirmative-action measures meant to level the playing field for black schoolchildren after a legacy of racism. The malleability of contemporary antiracist talk is perhaps most striking when Trump can claim that he is the least racist person in the world. Relying on the idea that racism is simply a matter of despising black people, he claims that he loves "blacks" and wants nothing more than for them to succeed.

Treating antiracism simply as an abstract philosophical orientation that names an honest refusal to be racist gives validity to all these expressions of antiracism. But rhetorical antiracism cheapens its historical meaning and specific political ideas. Without question, antiracism can be many things because it has no singular political ideology. But never has antiracist thought and action been entirely abstract and devoid of context for its practitioners who have held its banner in the struggle for racial liberation in US history. Antiracism's meaning, I argue, is found in this history. And my use of *antiracism* has a far more radical meaning than is appreciated today. Few Americans who today claim antiracism have even dared to accept such a radical vision because doing so would fundamentally change American politics.

I argue that the antiracist political tradition is defined by a rigorous political philosophy and mode of direct political engagement that provides an exemplary model for tackling racism in all forms.[5] Essential to the tradition is a direct and ongoing confrontation with the philosophy of racism, the individuals who embrace its ideas, and the structures and institutions that perpetuate it. Neglecting this history is politically misguided for those who claim to continue its struggle.[6]

Antiblack racism has always been antiracism's central focus[7]—not because it is more morally salient than other forms of racial oppression, such as anti-Semitism, Islamophobia, and anti-Latino racism, but because it has been the most expansive, historically durable, and salient form in America dating back almost four hundred years, since the first enslaved Africans arrived in Jamestown, Virginia, in

1619. In fact, adopting antiblack racism has become one way that many nonblack immigrants have tried to assimilate as white (in the nineteenth century, it was the Irish, Jews, Poles, Italians, and Germans, and today it is Latinos and Arab Americans).[8]

Strikingly, prevailing cultural and academic understandings of antiracism typically focus on white Americans at the expense of those who have offered the most sustained critique and vision of what racism is and how to dismantle it: black Americans.[9] Notwithstanding the recent burgeoning interest in African American political thought and the desire to expand the meaning of the American political tradition beyond its canonical white figures over the past few decades, black antiracist thought has not been given its full due.[10]

Antiracism recalls figures such as the militant white abolitionist John Brown, whose failed raid of Harper's Ferry, Virginia, in 1859 to liberate enslaved people was one of the major catalysts for the Civil War. Largely ignored, however, is the radical abolitionist David Walker, whose *Appeal to the Coloured Citizens of the World* (1829) called for direct struggle against racism by any means necessary; such statements placed a bounty on his head. Scholars have spent a great deal of energy examining the significance of Henry David Thoreau's refusal to pay taxes as a protest against slavery and the Mexican-American War of 1846. But they have insufficiently explored Anna Julia Cooper, who in *A Voice from the South* (1892) argued for the importance of black women's equality when doing so ran against all forms of male domination. Ralph Waldo Emerson, who claimed that slavery was inconsistent with democracy, is the subject of many critical studies in various academic fields, but marginalized is Malcolm X, who argued in the 1960s that racism was deeply entrenched in American hearts and minds when doing so made him public enemy number one. In many documentaries and high-school history textbooks, white Freedom Riders and white civil rights protestors are celebrated for joining hands with the black leaders of the civil rights movement, but save for the most notable figures such as King and Rosa Parks, too often overlooked are the hundreds of thousands of ordinary black people who marched in the streets. Today, white allies who have "Black Lives Matter!" posters on their front yards are heralded as exemplary patriots by other white people. But neglected are the young black men and women who take to the streets when their lives are existentially threatened by the possibility of police brutality and white terrorism.

Focusing on white antiracism is understandable because committed allies from the majority have always been crucial symbolically and politically to facilitate political change. But overlooking the political and philosophical contributions of the black antiracist tradition is a serious mistake. Black antiracists have had the most to gain and the most to lose and, time and time and time again, have demonstrated how to successfully challenge racism and racial inequality.

In this book, I provide an introduction to the antiracist intellectual legacy and its political movements in the US.[11] Antiracist critique, citizenship, and action are my sites of analysis. Intellectual history is my method. Contemporary political relevance is placed over abstract philosophical argument. Unifying principles across the tradition are highlighted above incommensurable differences. Major intellectual figures, movements, and core themes are placed above a comprehensive analysis of antiracism's everyday manifestations. This book is not a comprehensive systematic interpretation of the link between various black political ideologies and the antiracist tradition. A book like that remains to be written, but this book is more concerned with acquainting contemporary readers with a political theoretical tradition whose political legacy still remains obscured, if not forgotten.

I hope in this short book to go a small way toward recovering the antiracist imagination for all to appreciate. My argument is that by remembering antiracism historically, we can help refresh antiracist politics today. Regrettably, few political endeavors are timelier or more necessary.[12]

Strategies of Political Confrontation

For antiracists, abstract metaphysical arguments mattered less than political ones that could move people to action. Confronting arbitrary power mattered more than simply theorizing it, even though the two went hand in hand. A sense of history and a realistic interpretation of limitation and possibility mattered more than ideological purity, although antiracist idealistic claims themselves usually exceeded what seemed possible or even practical at the time. Antiracists expanded the meaning of *politics*—from compromise and realistic concessions meant to advance an agenda to the power struggle about what compromise obscures and what is, in fact, realistic.

Antiracists made their arguments in a wide range of ways. Fiction helped gave vivid expression to theoretical truths. Film gave visceral texture, while painting and visual art evoked powerful thoughts and ideas. Poetry and song crystallized core philosophical maxims. Political treatises deduced arguments, while emotional speeches moved publics from passivity to action. Some antiracists were activists, others writers—some both, while others neither. Women were as prevalent as men, although their contributions were often unacknowledged because of patriarchal commitments found in some important male antiracists. For many antiracists, politics and aesthetics were fused. Antiracist art dramatized political ideas. But antiracist politics were a kind of art. Public marches, symbolic protests, sit-ins, signs, chants, turns of phrase, metaphors, and narratives became creative strategies to make political arguments register broadly.[13]

How antiracists made their arguments is equally important. Rhetoric was a powerful weapon. Narratives sometimes juxtaposed opposing perspectives, sometimes blurred the lines between them, and sometimes textured what was implied or disavowed within them. The genre of romance, which stressed the themes of painless reconciliation and eventual triumph over tension and incommensurable differences, was often rejected by antiracists. But irony, and even comedy, helped dramatize inconsistencies, while tragedy revealed painful outcomes of seemingly innocuous choices. Autobiography helped give political authority. Moral conviction—whether founded in religion or humanism—provided a standpoint from which to vigorously criticize social injustice. Rarely did antiracists address hardened racists, but many nonetheless acted against violent and coercive racist institutions. Most addressed potentially sympathetic white allies but often sought to primarily politicize black citizens.[14]

Few antiracists consistently maintained the same positions over the course of their lives, and some even abandoned the project. Others supported many of the tradition's most important arguments, while some only took them in small doses at certain times. Nonetheless, black American antiracists had the most to say about the stakes for dismantling racism because they thought long and hard about it. Racism was part of the fabric of their lives. Black people were therefore often antiracism's central audience, but never did the vast majority of antiracists argue that their ideas were only essentially accessible to black people or that whites could not listen in. To the contrary, the overarching goal for many antiracists was that the white majority should internalize and embody their most powerful arguments politically.

Philosophical Roots

Antiracist political thought did not emerge ex nihilo. Philosophically, it took intellectual sustenance from, but ultimately pushed against, the modern political theoretical tradition alongside which it developed. Political modernity is generally associated with white, western European figures such as

Thomas Hobbes, John Locke, Karl Marx, G. W. F. Hegel, and Jean-Jacques Rousseau, all of whom embraced universal reason, called for historical progress, and defended the ideals of equality and freedom.[15] Antiracists thus exemplified what some scholars call an "Afro-modern" tradition, which was born out of the black diaspora struggle against enslavement worldwide. Afro-modernity challenged singular narratives of modernity while exposing as partial the invention of Euro-modernity.[16] Social identity for antiracists was understood to be constructed in ways that Euro-modernity did not fully appreciate—through myths and narratives about human value, about who counted and did not—rather than simply through political institutions. Antiracists believed that the construction of social identity also happened in ways more broadly than Euro-moderns did: not simply a rational process but an emotional, unconscious, and sometimes unintentional one. History for antiracists also became a crucial source of political change but was retold in more complex ways than Euro-moderns appreciated: as moving in ebbs and flows, in cycles that challenged easy notions of progress and linear time.

Various liberal political ideas associated with the American tradition were often put in the service of making antiracist arguments. But the meaning of these ideas was usually radicalized or reimagined. Rarely did antiracists begin their analysis with the so-called state of nature, a prepolitical state free from identity, hierarchy, and defined by perfect freedom. State-of-nature arguments gave liberal thinkers such as John Locke and later John Rawls, who defended what he called the "original position," as a way to legitimize political institutions and to think about justice.[17] But antiracist thought was much more grounded in lived experience. Inequality and domination became conditions from which antiracists theorized emancipation. And structural constraint was placed above celebrating individual willpower and freedom. This is why many antiracists thought that political rights required active protection from government and that equality demanded socioeconomic resources. Freedom was not about protection from government interference but the right to flourish, to love, to enjoy, and to live a good life. Democracy depended on spaces that allowed for self-governance in many spheres of life, rather than simply the right to vote and free and fair elections.[18]

Antiracism emerged from black American political thought but never expressed a singular political ideology.[19] Nonetheless, a shared set of ideas existed throughout the tradition. More liberal antiracists such as Frederick Douglass, Ida B. Wells, and Martin Luther King defended antiracist self-determination within their broader claims of preserving freedom through rights and dignity through law. Socialists such as T. Thomas Fortune, Hubert Harrison, and Fred Hampton defended the antiracist cultivation of networks of resistance around shared interests as part of their class-based arguments about confronting exploitative capitalism. Feminists such as Maria Stewart, Anna Julia Cooper, and Michele Wallace tethered black liberation to an end to violent and repressive patriarchy. But doing this extended the antiracist call for dismantling exploitative hierarchies and granted legitimacy to marginalized voices and perspectives. Although nationalists such as Martin R. Delany, Amiri Baraka, and Malcolm X believed black freedom could be best achieved through self-governing black-led communities, they continued the antiracist tradition by highlighting the way racism structured American society extensively. Participatory democrats such as the members of the Student Nonviolent Coordinating Committee (SNCC), Fannie Lou Hamer, and Ella Baker defended an antiracist theory of equality when arguing that black citizenship would be best expressed through direct, popular participation. Queer theorists such as James Baldwin and Audre Lorde, who defended LGBT liberation, troubled the meaning of what was socially normal and acceptable—within the larger antiracist framework of understanding that equality was always an unfinished project, demanding vigilance and constant struggle.

Against Conservatism

From a historical perspective, antiracist struggles were always waged somewhere within, or to the left of, political liberalism—socialism, communism, feminism, radical democracy, black power, pan-Africanism. To put it differently, rarely did antiracists wage their arguments or struggles in the name of conservatism.[20] And why would they? Conservatism had been central for justifying racism—think of slaveholders who said it was better to keep things the way they were because at least black people had food and shelter under slavery, or Jim Crow segregationists who said black people actually enjoyed and benefited from their racially segregated institutions.

Such conservative calls for the preservation of the status quo were always beneficial for the ruling class to keep its position—regardless of how and on whose backs and whose unpaid labor they gained it.[21] Not surprisingly, antiracist arguments about liberation opposed conservative ideals of gradual reform, established hierarchy, tradition, a return to the status quo, and nostalgia for the past.[22] Even more, antiracist commitments often opposed some conservative positions held by antiracists themselves. Frederick Douglass's support of federally led Reconstruction efforts suggested a much more forceful account of government intervention than his defense of a narrow version of black economic and political self-reliance. From the 1850s to the 1870s, Martin Delany's pragmatic attitude toward politics—by converting from a defender of black emigration to Canada and Central and South America after the passage of the Fugitive Slave Act (1850) to a major in the Union army during the Civil War and defender of the Reconstruction effort in the South— suggested the intellectual orientation for reconsidering his own masculinist faith in the virtues of benevolent male rule. Even Barack Obama's theory of history, which testified to the effect of racism on black socioeconomic opportunities, undercut his conservative claim that black people were culturally responsible for uplifting themselves from poverty. He said that black people need to take "full responsibility for our own lives—by demanding more from our fathers, and spending more time with our children. . . . They must never succumb to despair or cynicism; they must always believe that they can write their own destiny," at the same time that he stressed that "a lack of economic opportunity . . . and the lack of basic services . . . all helped create a cycle of violence, blight and neglect that continue to haunt us."[23]

One could find kernels of antiracist thought buried within a generally conservative framework. A critique of white supremacy as morally and politically degrading existed alongside Booker T. Washington's view of black self-help and racial accommodation.[24] An antiracist vision could be found in the fiction and essays of George Schuyler, who, before becoming an arch anticommunist in the postwar period and authoring *Black and Conservative* (1966), was a devout socialist in the 1920s and 1930s.[25]

But not only has conservatism never focused its attention on combating racism politically. More often than not, it has promulgated arguments conducive to perpetuating racial inequality. The onetime black civil rights activist James Meredith exhibited antiracist action by walking among a sea of white faces to desegregate the University of Mississippi in 1962. But there was nothing antiracist about Meredith eventually supporting the white supremacist David Duke's failed run for Louisiana governor in 1991. In Meredith's words, Duke's ultraconservative agenda—of cutting social welfare, advocating for white separatism, and speaking of black cultural inferiority—was refreshing because, at least, it was honest. "Whatever he said in years past," Meredith said, "he didn't say it behind our backs. And what he says today, we need to hear it. We all need to hear it. The liberals will be surprised how much of the black vote he receives."[26] More-over, the black neurosurgeon and current secretary of Housing and Urban Development (HUD), Ben Carson, repeated a classic racist trope by describing the horrific slave journey across the Middle Passage as similar to the waves of European immigrants arriving on American shores in search of economic opportunity. Carson supports Trump's policy of eliminating affordable housing, on which many black citizens depend, and this change has been evinced through HUD's striking out of "inclusive" and "free from discrimination" from its mission statement.[27] But Carson's argument is that black people today are descendants of earlier black dreamers, who were driven by a deep American patriotism centered around hard work. "That's what America is about, a land of dreams and opportunity," Carson said. "There were other immigrants who came here in the bottom of slave ships, worked even longer, even harder for less. But they too had a dream that one day . . . [their families] might pursue prosperity and happiness in this land."[28]

Historically, antiracist opposition was centered on racist ideas of the ruling class, whether it was rabid white supremacists such as the Ku Klux Klan after the Civil War or some racist white abolitionists before them, the political elite such as president Andrew Johnson in the 1860s or ordinary lynchers in the 1890s, self-described nonracist moderates who silently abetted the system in the 1960s during the civil rights movement, or radical communists or sympathetic liberals throughout the twentieth century who intentionally put the issue on the backburner. Antiracists also never shied away from attacking ostensibly progressive political ideas that claimed to support black freedom but did the opposite. Consider nineteenth-century calls for black emigration to Liberia and post-civil-rights talk of "color blindness," of not considering racial identity as a salient feature in addressing racial inequality.

Antiracism thus consistently countered the reactionary racist backlash it encountered—whether slaveholders' assault on abolitionism, white terrorism after Reconstruction, the recent assault on black freedom through talk of "reverse discrimination," or the view that postracialism has been achieved in the post-civil-rights era. But antiracists knew that backlash was something that required new strategies and coalitions, which needed to be refreshed through new thoughts within changing historical circumstances. Antiracists were thus closer to pragmatists than absolutists in responding to shifting realities, changing demographics, and new political coalitions. They were closer to realists in assessing and engaging the nature of political power, even though their idealism determined what counted as valuable and meaningful in politics. Solidifying this position meant engaging in public acts of protest—which meant adopting discomfort and vulnerability and appealing to fellow citizens.

Antiracist Thought and Resistance

New visions of citizenship that challenged racism were crucial too. Probing self-examination to eliminate one's complicity in promoting injustice was the antiracist response to the prevailing American innocence and disavowal that allowed racism to continue. Attentiveness to social construction overturned the racist embrace of essentialism—that black inequality was naturally supported by biology and culture. A vision of equality that was centered on promoting freedom in as many spheres as possible in both national and global contexts offered antiracists a way to oppose the limited definition advanced by racists and nationalists—as something only for whites, where justice meant "just us."

From abolitionism to the contemporary Movement for Black Lives, collective political movements became the central way antiracists demanded concessions from existing political power. Disruptive collective action became its most effective tactic. Exploiting divisions within political elites and party coalitions, while ensuring that emancipatory arguments were not made stale through intellectual stagnation and top-down leadership, was its most effective strategy. Transforming failure into rejuvenation and recognizing the failures within rejuvenation was its crucial philosophical orientation.

To be sure, not all antiracists were small-d democrats, but their ideas often aligned with the sensibility behind democracy (rule by the people) of self-determination and popular power. Most believed that people should be given freedom to make autonomous choices about the fate of their lives, that this project could not be easily settled through laws, and that elite power was often suspect and sometimes a bad substitute for the knowledge of ordinary people.[29] In this way, the antiracist sensibility was also closer to antiauthoritarianism because unchecked authority and arbitrary power are the first steps toward violence against the most vulnerable. Antiracists were also closer to social democrats than to libertarians because they knew that the idea of unfettered choice unconstrained by social reality propagated unsustainable dreams of social and economic competition, which fractured solidarity between potential allies.[30]

An Antiracist Sensibility

Antiracism always depends on asking several questions. Does it give power to those who have been the object of racism? Does it diminish unnecessary suffering in terms acceptable to those who are seeking dignity and emancipation, rather than those who benefit from the status quo? Is it done through collaboration rather than decree? Does it consider the plurality of experiences, identities, and needs and the way they can be overlooked? Is it flexible and receptive to contingency or closed off from it? Is it attentive to its own vulnerabilities?

Political strategy is important to antiracists. Some of the questions they asked were, Should we boycott now or later? Do we make coalitions with autoworkers, farmers, and prison guards? Should we advocate for greater regulation, more rights in the workplace, or autonomous, self-sustaining communities? Should we advocate for racial separatism or integration? But antiracists never sacrificed antiracism for larger political movements that adherents claimed were more pressing and required action more immediately.

A historical sensibility about antiracist political thought clarifies what is and is not a closer approximation of its practice. Certain forms of political engagement embody its spirit much more fully than others. Movement for Black Lives activists better exemplify it through calling for an end to police brutality than do American corporations whose corporate diversity programs focus on hiring black managers, while ignoring the economic well-being of the vast majority of their workforce. Making antiracist statements matters, but infinitely less than supporting antiracist policies that change structures. Teachers constructing curriculums stressing the formative role of racial inequality in American history do important antiracist work. But conservatives who call for cutting social programs because of their desire to end black dependency on them are as "antiracist" as slaveholders who said that keeping black people enslaved comes from their deep compassion for black people's health. Nothing is antiracist about action that keeps black people in a state of precariousness and domination. For this reason, Trump's self-professed antiracist intentions are belied by his embrace of white nationalism and moral equivalency between neo-Nazis and counterprotestors in Charlottesville—not to mention his doubling down on "law and order" talk, his executive order banning people from majority-Muslim countries, and much, much more.

From the antiracist perspective, denouncing Trump's racism is better than staying silent. But it pales in comparison to agitating for legislation and public policies that realize an-

tiracist dreams of freedom. Focusing on structural changes
is more important than individual or interpersonal transformations. Ending mass incarceration and police brutality is
better than efforts at racial reconciliation. Addressing racial
disparities in wealth through policies of socioeconomic redistribution is better than shopping in black-owned busi-
nesses. Eliminating the education gap through more public
funding of segregated schools is better than white people
moving into all-black neighborhoods. Never are these activities mutually exclusive, but those that address structures are
better—not for philosophical or moral reasons but because
history shows that they have worked in the past and broadly
affect more people.[31]

Antiracists who support these policies globally and understand the interconnection between racial liberation at
home and abroad embody more elements of the tradition
than those who harbor latent sexism and homophobia and
have sheer contempt for ordinary people. Equally crucial is
being mindful of contradiction. Good intentions can have
unintended consequences—white people gentrifying black
neighborhoods can lead to exploding home prices that push
the most vulnerable black citizens out. Ongoing reevaluation
should be embraced over ideological purity and perfect re-
sults. Nothing has been treated with more suspicion in the
tradition than the view that antiracism is easy to achieve.
More so than anything else, antiracism has imagined itself as
a horizon for thinking politically. Politics exists in a nonideal
world. An improvisatory attitude is necessary.

Antiracism and Its Critics

In response to conservatives who say that antiracism is too shrill in its assertions, too oppositional in its worldview, and too dangerous in its insistence on widespread equality, antiracists issue a simple answer.[32] Moderation means suffering, if not death, for the losers of the status quo. Time is something racism's beneficiaries can waste or stretch out ad infinitum but its victims want to condense as quickly as possible. Black people could not afford to wait when their lives were consumed by the ever-present threat of white terrorism in places such as Montgomery, Selma, and Birmingham and throughout much of the Deep South during Jim Crow or the devastating economic inequality and de facto segregation up north.

Anticipated within antiracist thought too is the left-wing critique. Radicals argue that focusing on racism is nothing more than an exclusionary form of identity politics, which sacrifices the economic liberation of all working-class people throughout the world for the immediate, feel-good, but shallow claims of recognition from victimized groups.[33] From the antiracist perspective, not only is this a misdiagnosis of the problem and a false choice politically, but it also comes from mutually exclusive reasoning. Economic inequality and capitalism certainly perpetuate racism, but racism relies on so much more beyond class—fantasy, myth, narrative, and unconscious emotion and social definition. A class-conscious utopia offers no magic fix for racism. To the contrary, dismantling racism and economic inequality go hand in hand. Opposing instrumentalism and dehumanization, on which both racism and exploitative capitalism depend, was always central to antiracism. Ignoring this link means engaging in reasoning that sustains exploitation in all forms—a reasoning that sees struggle as based in singular choices against some order that will persist forever. Antiracists know that exploitative orders have histories, so their futures are far from certain. What matters is the will to challenge them.

The Urgency of Antiracism

Antiracism is important now. The question is not what can be done but who will be willing to do it. Racism is alive and well today. Trump's election in 2016 was emblematic of this fact. Since his campaign began in 2015, racist hate crimes have been on the rise and growing, creating even more precariousness for people of color.[34] Anti-immigrant racism has had a new lease on life. Those who are perceived to be Arab American, even when they are not, are deemed de facto terrorists. For many white Americans, beards, turbans, hijabs, and burkas reflect an uncontrollable submission to a violent philosophy of jihadism. Trump's administration is more persistent in its Islamophobia than those before it—as was evident through his travel ban on citizens of seven majority-Muslim nations, which, before suffering defeats in public opinion, on the streets, and in the lower courts, was recently upheld by a slim five-to-four conservative majority in the US Supreme Court. Also, Latinos are seen as the source of the US opioid epidemic—bringing crate loads of drugs illegally across the US-Mexico border to poison innocent white

Americans—and as forcing white people to adopt Spanish as a second language. Further indication that Trump's nativism is here to stay comes from his recent reversal of the popular Obama-era program DACA (Deferred Action for Childhood Arrivals), which protects young, undocumented migrants from deportation and gives them the opportunity to go to school and earn a living.

A narrow focus on Trump's victory, however, obscures that for black Americans there has been much of the same since the end of the civil rights movement and the dismantling of Jim Crow segregation—even after the election of the first black president, twice. Racist arguments persist to justify racist structures. Mass incarceration and police brutality, which disproportionately affect black Americans, are described as a consequence of black delinquency. Black educational inequality is seen as a product of black irreverence toward adopting upstanding norms of citizenship. Black poverty is seen as a consequence of bad personal choices—of having children out of wedlock, doing drugs, being careless toward one's neighborhood, and living off government social benefits.[35] What this view implies is that black citizens occupy a lower rung on the normative social order; they are just not that good and not deserving of being taken seriously.[36]

This condition seems dire. But antiracism provides political hope today. Remembering the longevity and persistence of antiracism in America should encourage those who are struggling with profound pessimism, who are hopeless about a nonracist future. Antiracists tell us that struggle matters. Remembering that American antiracism emerged on US shores challenges the view that America exists only in the hands of those who dominate, who oppress, who have no problem inflicting suffering. The powerful are powerful for a reason, but they are not invincible. When power is tested, it becomes less self-assured. Inequality will not easily disappear, but it can be diminished. Remembering antiracism is ultimately about reclaiming a new future in which a multiracial democracy is possible, in which racism does not promote war, genocide, environmental collapse, economic inequality, and sexual violence.

Racism has evolved in new ways, but so too have our times. Demographic shifts, which show that white Americans will soon be just one—albeit powerful—minority among many, are re-creating the meaning of American identity. Younger people are becoming less overtly racist and more willing to accept multicultural democracy. Socialist ideas about economic equality, which even a decade ago would have seemed pipe dreams, if not overtly anti-American, have been revived and embraced by millions of people. Nothing demonstrated this more than the insurgent 2016 presidential campaign of Senator Bernie Sanders of Vermont, who won 43 percent of the popular vote in the Democratic primaries. Social media is connecting people in faster and more significant ways, while activist groups are sprouting throughout the globe.

Rapid political changes, long in the making, seem to be happening before our eyes. Most obvious is the fracturing of the Republican Party coalition—the network of religious conservatives, free-market libertarians, and war-hawk neoconservatives—that has been held together since Ronald

Reagan's presidency in the 1980s and saw its high-water mark during the presidency of George W. Bush. Never was there any truth to Trump's populist campaign pledge to maintain what little was left of the social welfare state in the Social Security, Medicaid, and Medicare programs. But his shrewd argument was as much as anything else a product of the waning Republican influence on public opinion.

A similar political upheaval is under way in mainstream American liberalism. After Hillary Clinton's stunning loss in the 2016 presidential election, Democrats find themselves with no fresh political vision—stuck between their fidelity to corporate interests and their fervent anti-Trumpism, which is, too often, less a political critique about undemocratic inequality and more a moralistic one about inadequate presidential etiquette. Not all of these transformations guarantee progressive change, nor are they intrinsically emancipatory without people to enact them. But as in the past, there is tremendous opportunity for antiracists to link their unique political vision with, and in ways that deepen, other liberation moments aiming to create a better future.

The structure of this book is as follows. Chapter 2 examines how antiracists reimagine the meaning, underpinnings, and persistence of, and thus oppose, American racism and racial inequality. Chapter 3 charts the antiracist freedom vision and theory of citizenship. Chapter 4 examines the way antiracist ideas created antiracist political movements, which entailed tactics and strategies to confront structural racial inequality. And chapter 5 argues that antiracist political thought and struggle can energize our politics today.

2

Rejecting the Power of Racism

Antiracists define racism as based not in nature but in arbitrary power—the right to suppress, exclude, demean, disauthorize, and degrade people—based on what the twentieth-century queer feminist poet Audre Lorde called the presumptive "right to dominance."[1] A now-classic definition was further provided by black power advocates Kwame Ture (formerly Stokely Carmichael) and Charles Hamilton in their book *Black Power* (1967): "By 'racism' we mean the predication of decisions and policies on considerations of race for the purpose of *subordinating* a racial group and maintaining control over that group. . . . Racism is both covert and overt. It takes two, closely related forms: individual whites acting against individual blacks, and acts by the total white community against the total black community."[2] Antiracists understood that naming racism was as essential as avoiding philosophical abstractions in understanding its inner workings. Power disparities, rather than simply people's individual intentions or feelings toward others, are central to racism. By stressing the way racism works through subordination and control, antiracists rejected the idea that all racial groups were equally capable of demeaning behavior.

To be sure, sometimes antiracists themselves fell prey to, or reproduced arguments that bore a striking similarity to, racism. For instance, Frederick Douglass supported the annexation to the US of Santo Domingo in 1871. Though his decision was arguably more pragmatic—based in the desire to include more black citizens into the US polity—than it was based in white supremacy, his view was that Santo Domingo's citizens were "weak and defenceless" and that annexation would give them a "healthy activity."[3]

Though the antilynching activist Ida B. Wells's primary desire was to instill a sense of outrage in white citizens, she perpetuated anti–Native American racism when she said, "The red Indian of the Western plains tied his prisoner to the stake, tortured him, and danced in fiendish glee while his victim writhed in the flames. His savage, untutored mind suggested no better way than that of wreaking vengeance upon those who had wronged him."[4] Almost a century later, the Black Arts poet Amiri Baraka was accused of anti-Semitism. Even though the poetic speaker of his controversial poem about the September 11, 2001, attacks on the World Trade Center, "Somebody Blew Up America," explicitly denounced the horrors of the Holocaust by saying, "Who put the Jews in ovens / and who helped them do it," he also perpetuated the conspiracy that the Israeli state had prior knowledge about the 2001 attack: "Who knew the World Trade Center was gonna get bombed / Who Told 4000 Israeli Workers at the Twin Towers / To stay home that day."[5]

But all antiracists believed that historical context matters. Just because black citizens could embrace racist ideas did not mean that they had historically been the ones to put these ideas into practice on a mass scale politically. To put it succinctly, racist ideas in the US have been unleashed by white people to dominate black people, not the other way around. Black people never enslaved millions of white people or lynched three thousand white men or segregated school-children in public schools.

But the primary target of antiracist attack was not white people. Instead, it was always the racist ideology of inherent white superiority, or "white supremacy," and the coercive institutions it authorized. Antiracists have almost always conceptualized racism systematically. For instance, the nineteenth-century abolitionist David Walker hoped that white people could become moral Christians but reserved his greatest ire for slavery, what he called an "inhuman system."[6] The civil rights activist Martin Luther King Jr. criticized white segregationists but had as his primary focus the "evil system" of Jim Crow.[7] The contemporary prison abolitionist Angela Davis has criticized innocent Americans who justify disproportionate mass incarceration but has focused her organizing efforts on dismantling this "rotten system" through cultivating democratic social movements.[8]

This is why antiracists have usually defined racism as a political construction of social reality, rather than a natural occurrence.[9] "Political" means a power struggle over what resources and punishments people get, what knowledge is privileged, who counts as human, and who is morally valuable or abject.[10] Antiracists advance three theses to define racism. The first is that racism is created through human action. The second is that racism is a condition of power, defined by hierarchy and superiority/inferiority. The third is that racism is defined by privileging certain knowledge and perspectives while denigrating others.

These three arguments are concretized by the contemporary visual artist Kara Walker in *"Slavery! Slavery!* (1997). Black silhouettes positioned against a white backdrop render clear the painstaking process through which the black-white binary that racism claims to be permanent is always undoing itself through black life. Black agency is expressed in Walker's work through the basic fact of ordinary people living despite the specter of white power and physical weapons of coercion lurking in the background. The idea of racism being a political construction was behind the nineteenth-century black emigrationist (as well as novelist, physician, and statesman) Martin R. Delany's argument that racism was a matter of historical chance rather than fate, in his classic text *The Condition, Elevation, Emigration and Destiny of the Colored People* (1852). Responsibility for slavery was not black biological inferiority, he insisted, but that the powerful exploited the weak, who were "the *least potent* in urging their claims."[11] The nineteenth-century black antislavery activist David Walker, who wrote in *Freedom's Journal* and was a salesman of used clothing in Boston, agreed with Delany. Decades earlier, he said that Africans were not made "for nothing else but to dig their mines and work their farms. . . . [Those who believe this] cannot believe history, sacred or profane."[12] In different ways, antiracists exposed what racists denied: racism is a contingent form of power—it is evolving, shifting, and self-renewing in unexpected ways.

One central way antiracists believed racism evolved was through a racialized construction of citizenship. Criminalizing black political dissent as inherently un-American is what the antilynching activist T. Thomas Fortune saw when black protest against white terrorism was treated with suspicion during Reconstruction: "The newspapers of the country, voicing the sentiments of the people, literally hiss into silence any man who has the courage to protest against the prevailing tendency to lawlessness."[13] Photographs capturing massive white resistance to school desegregation revealed this dynamic to James Baldwin. The crowd of enraged white students spitting on the black student Dorothy Counts as she walked to Harding High School in Charlotte, North Carolina, in 1957 could not imagine Counts fighting for her rights, could not see that she was enacting exemplary democratic citizenship. What they saw instead was a threat. Antiracists such as Fortune and Baldwin knew that black activism reinforced racism, which is to say that the more black citizens protested the injustice of their condition, the more enraged white people became. In their view, white people came to believe that black dissent confirmed black irreverence for upstanding citizenship, for civility and good behavior. Consequently, the white response was to reclaim without any serious critical examination a white public sphere that was being questioned by a burgeoning black public. "The South," Baldwin wrote, "clings to its past, but it is being, meanwhile, inexorably changed by an entirely unmythical present. . . . This is why there is such panic at the bottom and such impotence on top."[14]

A crucial way antiracists made their arguments was by both questioning existing political authority and seizing it for themselves. The nineteenth-century feminist abolitionist Sojourner Truth's rhetorical question "ain't I a woman?" (1851) delivered at the Women's Convention in Akron, Ohio, presupposed what Baldwin argued in 1964: "the humanity of the submerged population is equal to the humanity of anyone else, equal to yours, equal to that of your child."[15] There is a long history of antiracists *disproving* racist arguments about black biological and cultural inferiority—for instance, Ida B. Wells debunked the myth of black male hypersexuality, used to justify lynching, by revealing how interracial intimacy was often consensual rather than forced, while Du Bois in *The Philadelphia Negro* (1899) used sociological evidence to explain socioeconomic racial inequality. Many antiracists, however, avoided the trap of proving that black people were *really* human beings. They presumed, rather than defended, black equality, which became the standpoint from which to say that racial inequality was a fundamental distortion. David Walker questioned in his *Appeal* (1829) whether it was possible to assume Thomas Jefferson's commitment to equality when his racist reasoning in "Query XIV" in his classic book *Notes on the State of Virginia* (1781) held that black people were morally inferior. Walker wondered, "Had I not rather die, or be put to death, than to be a slave to any tyrant, who takes not only my own, but my wife and children's lives by the inches? Yea, would I meet death . . . in preference to such *servile submission* to the murderous hands of tyrants. . . . The charges of Mr. Jefferson [are thus] refuted by the blacks *themselves*."[16]

Stressing black political agency allowed antiracists to turn the tables on white people and stress power inequality as the key explanation for racism. As Baldwin asked, "Why do you need a 'nigger'?"[17]

Different answers were given to Baldwin's question, but few antiracists believed that racism was entirely irrational. Racism is functional. Some antiracists believed it provides a powerful psychological antidote to the existential white fear of social failure. Ordinary people get power in a world over which they have little control. As W. E. B. Du Bois famously explained in his classic *Black Reconstruction in America* (1935), "the white group of laborers, while they received a low wage, were compensated in part by a powerful public and psychological wage."[18] Thus, undermined throughout much antiracist thought were uncomplicated progressive calls for class-conscious utopias. Increasing white vulnerability did not mean that there would be action against economic inequality. To the contrary, the anger experienced by whites was redirected toward black people. Du Bois and Cyril Briggs in particular held that the economic elite's mobilization of racism, what Hubert Harrison called "cast prejudice," eroded working-class interracial solidarity to boost profits.[19] Only some antiracists were devout Marxists or socialists, but most agreed that racist exploitation—not simply hard work—created American prosperity. Slave labor made the American Dream of upward mobility and material wealth; as Du Bois put it in *The Gift of Black Folk* (1924), anticipating Baldwin, "[The Negro's] labor was foundational to American prosperity."[20]

Many antiracist texts rejected US democracy's claim of immunity from racism. Frederick Douglass disagreed with abolitionists influenced by the editor of the *Liberator*, William Lloyd Garrison, who held that the Constitution was ultimately a slaveholding document. But Douglass still conceded—as did many antiracists before and after—that the US system of checks and balances and separation of powers allowed the framers to label black people three-fifths of a person and for slaveholding states to remain.[21] States'-rights arguments, which claimed to promote self-rule for southern states after Reconstruction, according to Ida Wells, gave lynchers freedom to invalidate the rights of black people, who were "hung by midnight raiders, and openly murdered in the light of day. . . . The franchise vouchsafed to the Negro grew to be a 'barren ideality.'"[22] A definition of justice as the rule of the most powerful, in which, as Wells put it, "might makes right," explained why white people felt such violence to be their prerogative.[23]

Racism and American Political Culture

Varying levels of optimism existed within antiracist thought about whether Americans were truly committed to the ideals in the Declaration of Independence and Constitution. But many antiracists implicated in racism's perpetuation the very American cultural ideals believed to oppose it. In "A Letter from Birmingham Jail" (1963), King's faith in racial progress coexisted with his recognition that treating it as an unquestioned fact enabled white moderates to ignore black suffering.[24] Collective uplift for racial liberation was defended by nineteenth-century antiracists but was also used for white racial paternalism. For example, the American Colonization Society (ACS), founded in 1816 and supported by figures such as Henry Clay, James Madison, and Thomas Jefferson, wanted to send enslaved people to Liberia as a solution to the problem of slavery. But many of its supporters and its key publication, *African Repository and Colonial Journal*, accepted the pernicious myths of black inferiority, leading figures such as David Walker to denounce it and Martin Delany to say that it was "anti-Christian in its character and misanthropic in its pretended sympathies" and would only serve to perpetuate black social marginalization in the US.[25]

The deadly effect of white goodwill was displayed in one of the landmarks of American cinema, Spike Lee's *Do the Right Thing* (1989). Lee's film was a critique of New York's new policy of "broken windows" policing, which focused on harsh responses to minor crime as a deterrent for more significant crime. And it detailed the failure of white liberalism. Throughout the film, Sal, a white, Italian American pizzeria owner, dotes on his black customers in the predominantly black neighborhood of Bedford-Stuyvesant in Brooklyn, New York, in the 1980s. But the film's conclusion reveals this attitude to be a distortion. After one of the black customers, "Radio Raheem," refuses to turn down his radio, playing Public Enemy's classic "Fight the Power," Sal enlists the power of a white police officer, who strangles Raheem to death.

Do the Right Thing showed how white goodwill was always conditional and had its limit—it demanded black people to be good paying customers, and socially respectable, or else they would be subject to severe punishment. Two decades earlier, Malcolm X had taken Lee's critique of American compassion in a different direction. In his autobiography (1965), Malcolm explained the way it could become the mechanism through which to assault and reverse black people's feelings of self-worth. Racism masqueraded as sensible realism when Malcolm's white teacher from his youth, Mr. Ostrowski, rejected Malcolm's desire to become a lawyer by saying, "now we all like you here, you know that, but you're a nigger, and a lawyer is no realistic goal for a nigger."[26]

The American idea of evolutionary change, rather than radical transformation, became the way that the US Supreme Court in *Brown v. Board of Education* (1954) could say that the Jim Crow South had a constitutional obligation to end school segregation "with all deliberate speed." Patience meant that desegregation could be done as quickly or slowly as was acceptable for whites. The critical race theorist and law scholar Derrick Bell was not surprised that massive white resistance to integration quickly ensued: the Supreme Court had set "a standard for compliance—the 'all deliberate speed' standard—that was so vague that it all but halted the implementation of the first *Brown* decision for at least fifteen years."[27] States did a number of things to slow integration: they relied on administrative arguments and blamed the bureaucracy, claimed limited economic resources and stressed the problem of legal ambiguity of what desegregation itself meant practically.

White Innocence and Disavowal

Rarely did antiracists insist that bad knowledge is a necessary condition for racism.[28] Ignorance, or the failure to understand or appreciate certain facts and truths, is just as important. Ignorance, however, was closely related to the problem of what antiracists called "racial innocence," which was less about knowing certain things and more about failing to give them moral weight or salience. When Baldwin saw the utter apathy with which white people treated black people living in inadequately resourced, segregated housing in cities across the US in the 1960s, he claimed that it was such "innocence" that "constitutes the crime."[29]

Consequently, antiracists rejected arguments that narrowly assigned racism to obviously very bad actors—white supremacists, neo-Nazis, Klansmen, and white nationalists. They knew that sensationalizing bad actors exonerates the majority of decent people who—despite their awareness—are nonetheless responsible for keeping intact racial inequality. Antiracists thus focused their criticism on the white majority who sometimes tacitly and sometimes unknowingly embraced racist ideas. Unconscious racism—associations, beliefs, and narratives—gives tacit support to racial inequality. White people demean but deny demeaning. Claiming innocence of racism obscures conscious white choices while perpetuating unequal black dehumanization. This was captured through what Du Bois described as a formative experience in *The Souls of Black Folk* (1903) when he was denied recognition from a white playmate. The girl who refused to trade a card with him may not have said anything hurtful, but her neglect and look of utter contempt made Du Bois feel like he was "different from the others, . . . shut out from their world by a vast veil."[30]

Unconscious racism is also why progressive commitments never expunge racist beliefs. John Brown was a militant white abolitionist who believed he was black people's savior. Abraham Lincoln issued the Emancipation Proclamation in 1863 but defended white supremacy when he was first running for president. Opposition to institutions of racial domination is not identical to committed egalitarianism. This is what Audre Lorde said when black women's voices were excluded from white, middle-class feminist organizing against gender inequality in the 1970s and 1980s. Liberation for all women could not happen when the feminist movement used the "master's tools" to "dismantle the master's house": "As white women ignore their built-in privilege of whiteness and define woman in terms of their own experience alone, then women of Color become 'other,' the outsider whose experience and tradition is too 'alien' to comprehend."[31]

Embedded in these examples is a crucial antiracist thesis. Racism does not hinge on racist words (*nigger*) or theories of biological determinism (that black people's genetic composition makes them morally and intellectually inferior to whites). Myths and descriptors unequally applied to black people are just as crucial. Today's language of "welfare queens," "inner city," "underclass," and "ghetto people" echoes the time-honored ideas that black people are, as the twentieth-century essayist and novelist Ralph Ellison once explained, "ignorant, cowardly, thieving, lying, hypocritical, . . . filthy of personal habit, sexually animalistic, crude and disgusting in their public content, and aesthetically just plain unpleasant."[32]

The antiracist knows that calling racist ideas "stereotypes" grants them unfounded legitimacy. Stereotypes generalize truths. But these are distortions that cannot possibly explain anything, because they encompass all social problems (crime, violence, ignorance, immorality) and because they project these problems onto a singular group of people, which cannot—on either an empirical or a philosophical level—possibly be held responsible for them and be seen as exceptionally expressing them at unequal rates to others. Baldwin captured this point when he said that to think of a black person is to "think of statistics, slums, rapes, injustices, remote violence . . . as though his continuing status among us were somehow analogous to disease, . . . which must be checked, even though it cannot be cured."[33] From Baldwin's vantage point, it seemed farcical, if not downright absurd, to speak of black citizens as being immoral or deviant, for it begged a host of questions: Isn't everyone sometimes immoral at times? Who exactly is immoral and for what specific reasons? How are black people more immoral than white people?

Nonetheless, that many good-intentioned white people continued to believe in these ideas—or fail to see them as a blatant and willful reliance on specious reasoning that endowed people with a superhuman negativity—led Malcolm X to insist that racism "has rooted itself so deeply in the subconsciousness of many American whites that they them-selves of times are not even aware of its existence."[34] A willful choice was at the heart of believing that black people could be the repository of social disaster.

Conjured in these associations is a wide range of emo-tions, defined by what Du Bois called "a deep and passion-ate hatred, vast by the very vagueness of its expressions."[35] Few antiracists thought that most white people were be-yond reformation, but virtually all treated with suspicion what many white moderates and reformers claimed to be easy: to persuade those who support racist ideas to abandon them, to reason with them, or to move them to see the folly of their ways.

Converting someone from racism to antiracism is hard because emotions created by racism disarm the rational com-munication and reflection necessary to expunge racism. Fear of imagined black criminals—in the words of Angela Davis, "young black men engender fear"—makes white Ameri-cans defend prison expansion.[36] Fear of black male sexuality makes them misunderstand that racial integration is not, as Ture and Hamilton put it, a matter of black people "want-ing to marry white daughters" but to "improve their lives—politically and economically."[37] Nowhere was the cycle of white rage and antiblack paranoia as powerfully expressed as in the Harlem Renaissance writer Nella Larsen's novel *Passing* (1929). "They give me the creeps. Those black scrimy devils," John Bellew says, even though he is a white man who is un-knowingly married to and has two interracial children with a black woman, Clare Kendry, who is passing as white: "Always robbing and killing people . . . And Worse."[38] Here is the vicious cycle that antiracists identify: rage inspires fear and violence and, ultimately, blinds one from recognizing it. After Bellew finds out Kendry's secret, he calls her a "dirty nigger," before she eventually falls to her death from an open window. Ultimately, this is as much a loss for him. What Bellew gains through white supremacy pales compared to what he loses by becoming a widower and a single parent to his two children. This was *Passing*'s version of antiracist prophetic critique. White people suffer from racism too.

From Walker to Douglass, King to Baldwin, who said "our dehumanization of the Negro then is indivisible from our dehumanization of ourselves,"[39] laying bare racism's dehumanizing effects on whites allowed antiracists to undo expectations of white immunity. Prophetic arguments excavated the existential and political consequences of racism. Many were intended to play on whites' moral conscience to move them to action—this was the hope behind the black liberation theologian James Cone's assertion that "racism is a disease that perverts one's moral sensitivity and distorts the intellect."[40] But others played on what they thought was more persuasive: shared interest. The prophetic meaning behind civil rights activists shouting "No Justice No Peace!" was not simply about foreshadowing black political agitation. It was also about stressing how racism desensitized American citizens to violence and created unintended blowback.

Integration and Exclusion

Spirited disagreements about racial integration and separatism existed within the antiracist tradition. But very few
antiracists thought cultural assimilation was the primary
solution to racism. Cultural assimilationism refers to the idea
that black equality can be achieved through more black people adopting so-called mainstream values—such as speaking
white American vernacular, not listening to rap music or hip
hop, adopting white names, not wearing hoodies, and dress-
ing "properly."

Malcolm X disagreed with King's view that agitation
needed to be couched in the theatrics of respectability. But
neither figure believed that black equality demanded that
black people become whiter. No text so vividly articulated
the impossibility of blacks' racial passing as white as George
Schuyler's Harlem Renaissance satirical novel *Black No
More* (1931). *Black No More* described the frantic way white
people would create racial distinctions after a "magical pro-
cedure" could make black people have white skin. Throughout the novel, white workers begin to look for the subtlest
attributes—a vernacular, a twitch of the eye, a prolonged
stare—to identify secret blacks. They begin to administer
genealogical tests to prove who genuinely has white ancestors, and in the final comedic twist—after virtually everyone
is physically white—those who are deemed to have "stained
skin" or are too pale become the targets of discrimination.
Black No More's narrator describes the novel's critique of
white moral panic in the following way: "There were fre-

quent reports in the daily press of white woman giving birth to black babies. . . . The entire nation became alarmed. . . . Every stranger was viewed with suspicion. . . . Chastity became a virtue. . . . Matrimony at last began to be approached with caution."[41]

A less satirical antiracist critique of assimilation was displayed in the play *Dutchman* (1964) by the leading figure of the Black Arts Movement, Leroi Jones (later Amiri Baraka). Only some antiracists agreed with Baraka's black cultural nationalism and militancy, but many would have been sympathetic to his view that black freedom would be thwarted insofar as white people have the final say on the meaning of black authenticity. *Dutchman* made this clear through an interracial exchange on a New York subway train between a black man, Clay, and a white woman, Lua, who, despite Clay's repeated refusals, successfully solicits him to realize her projected fantasies of black hypersexuality, patriarchal violence, and criminality, which he eventually does by slapping her. She tells him, "Come on, Clay. Let's rub bellies on the train. The nasty. The nasty. Do the gritty grind, like your ol' rage-head mammy. Grind till you lose your mind. Shake it, shake it! OOOOweeee! Come on, Clay."[42] But nothing transformative comes from Clay's ensuing educative monologue to the audience about white racism and its denial of black individuality. Rather than enact the myth of black violence and thus realize Lua's fantasies, Clay says, "I'd rather be a fool. Insane. Safe with my words, and no death, and clean, hard thoughts, urging me to new conquests."[43] Lua thus takes matters into her own hands, eventually stabbing to death both Clay and his respectability just as he is about to exit the train. Black people are either too black or insufficiently white. Nonexistent is the freedom to do what they want or act however they feel.

History and Structural Racial Inequality

One central antiracist argument has always been that even if white people cleansed racism from their minds, racial inequality would still persist. This is because collective institutions create inequality beyond individual feelings. Antiracists knew that structures have greater coercive power than individuals do. Structures are composed of complex written and unwritten rules, organizations, languages, methods, laws, and philosophical principles that promote injustice. The core antiracist question is always this: Are structures built on and worked through and do they help perpetuate the reality of the central racist assumption that black life is of a lesser value than white life?

Antiracists knew that racism and antiracism existed on an unequal playing field. Egalitarian laws could not eliminate racism, but racism could erode their power. To be sure, very few antiracists dismissed laws that promoted political rights or civil liberties—the right to vote, the right to free speech, the right to privacy, the right to be treated equally or to be protected from cruel and unusual punishment. But political rights were seen as limited in solving an accumulation of white-enacted historical racist injustice. Measurable socioeconomic consequences had effects long after the most hardened racists died and the most brutal racial institutions such as slavery fell. For Du Bois, slavery haunted the post-Reconstruction black southern community where he lived and taught. As he described it in *Souls*, "slavery was a dim recollection of childhood," but its ghost still haunted through the way black people had to experience "hardship in poverty, poor land, and low wages," which expressed the "Veil that hung between [them] and Opportunity."[44] Ironically, the figure who continued Du Bois's argument in the twenty-first century was the one who many people thought confirmed its rejection: Barack Obama. Postracialism and painless democratic achievement was impossible for the very antiracist reason that Obama himself articulated in a 2008 campaign speech in Philadelphia before he was elected, called "A More Perfect Union." He said, "Legalized discrimination—where blacks were prevented, often through violence, from owning property, or loans were not granted to African-American business owners, or black homeowners could not access FHA mortgages, or blacks were excluded from unions, or the police force, or fire departments—meant that black families could not amass any meaningful wealth to bequeath to future generations. That history helps explain the wealth and income gap between black and white, and the concentrated pockets of poverty that persists in so many of today's urban and rural communities."[45] Racist policies enacted or supported by federal and state government have a life of their own. Stolen black labor under slavery and, under Jim Crow, housing discrimination and ghettoization, welfare stigmatization, redlining, and the crafting of the GI Bill—which offered home loans and college opportunities to World War II veterans in ways that were unavailable to blacks—have consequences. They shape everything from black political opportunities, economic independence, and health outcomes to fairness in the criminal justice, legal equality, employment, and education.[46] The effect of this knowledge is clear. Racism's strategic weapon of defense is disarmed: blurring distinctions between victims and perpetrators. "Color blindness," in which white people claim that they do not make judgments based on race, is rejected as an antidote to racial injustice.[47] No longer is it possible to insist on the idea of rugged individualism, in which all people are imagined to fully control their destiny through personal choices and hard work. Attention to structural racial inequality undermines cultural pathology arguments. It is more difficult to claim that laziness "causes" black poverty when one sees the poorly funded, crumbling housing projects in which black people live. This is what Ture and Hamilton described as the problem with the "dark ghetto," which was "created by the lack of decent housing, decent jobs and adequate education."[48] Black immorality cannot explain mass incarceration when the criminal justice system's disproportionate incarceration of black people (even though white people do not commit any less, even if sometimes different kinds of, crime) over the past three decades shows that criminalization has nothing to do with increasing black crime. In the words of Angela Davis, "the structural racism of the prison system can be held responsible for the persistence of racism in the so-called free-world."[49]

Racism, Culture, and American Identity

An even more powerful antiracist claim has been that "culture" does not have much explanatory value for socio-economic inequality. This is because cultural explanations are predicated on the misguided assumption that culture is either pure or only consumed by its primary creators. To the contrary, argued the Harlem Renaissance philosopher Alain Locke, the black experience not only was defined through an immersion in American culture but had contributed to American culture "humor, sentiment, imagination and tropic nonchalance."[50] Something similar was said in Baraka's seminal *Blues People* (1963): "Africanisms are not limited to Black people, . . . but American culture itself . . . includes a great many Africanisms."[51] The antiracist implied this: How could white people be sure that their "values" are not themselves influenced by black people? How could black people's "culture" ever be fully divorced from the larger culture in which they live? From this, it follows that if black culture is somehow truly "pathological," then white people too are never immune from its consequences because they consume it at high rates. All this is why Ellison found it so absurd to see a white youngster singing along to music composed by a black musician, Stevie Wonder, while at the same time shouting "racial epithets at the black youngsters trying to swim at a public beach."[52] At the same time, it was equally absurd to insist on black cultural pathology because black cultural products such as the blues, jazz, and gospel generated values of resilience—what Cornel West called a "tragicomic hope," a "hope not hopeless but unhopeful,"[53] that sustained historic black struggle against racist marginalization.

More often than not, however, a core antiracist strategy was turning the table around to white Americans to ask, Is American culture not a culture of violence, criminality, and apathy, especially from the perspective of the American racist history of slavery and Jim Crow? It was more difficult to sustain unquestioned American morality when, in the words of the former Black Panther in the late 1960s H. Rap Brown, "violence was as American as cherry pie."[54] This made it harder for white Americans to insist that ethical values ultimately superseded domination. Progress was never guaranteed. If anything, this was more a utopian wish than a realistic assessment of the future—as the poetic speaker in Langston Hughes's poem "Let America Be America Again" (1938) put it, America was a "rack and ruin of . . . gangster death," made through "rape and rot of graft, and stealth, and lies."[55]

Antiracist perspective shifts thus dismantled romantic conceptions of American identity that insulated white Americans from critical self-examination and social transformation. Antiracists backed white innocents into a corner: either they had to renounce cultural explanations for black inequality or see themselves as complicit in both producing and embracing a "pathological" American culture that all Americans would be responsible for remaking.

The Life of Racism

But how did antiracists persuade Americans to remake the culture? For starters, they knew that it was fruitless to debate the morality of racial domination. Douglass said what almost all antiracists believed: "Must I argue that a system thus marked with blood, and stained with pollution, is *wrong*? No! I will not."[56] Implied here was that rational argument had limited persuasive success. It was necessary instead to shift the perspective from white to black lives and from a bird's-eye view to lived experience. Rarely did antiracists ask citizens to go to some imagined prepolitical, natural position where all were equal to think about justice—as was common in liberal thought.[57] Instead, they supplemented narratives of the lived experience of racism with asking white people to consider whether it would be acceptable to them. This is what motivated Du Bois to ask, "How does it feel to be a problem? . . . [It] is a strange experience,—peculiar even for one who has never been anything else,"[58] or Douglass to ask his audience to imagine the New Orleans slave market, where men were "examined like horses" and "the forms of women [were] rudely and brutally exposed to the shocking gaze of American slave-buyers."[59]

Such antiracist perspective shifts countered a core racist argument: that racism was never that bad. It is still common to hear that black people live in the greatest country on earth and have decent social programs. An analogous claim was made in the nineteenth century: enslaved people were fed and nourished, did not have to compete with white workers in a brutal system of capitalism, and were taught Christianity. The nineteenth-century defender of slavery John C. Calhoun said, "Never before has the black race . . . attained a condition so civilized and so improved, not only physically, but morally and intellectually."[60]

This interpretation became less sustainable when racism's vast deprivation was visibly exposed. Black people were forced to labor without pay, beaten, and demoralized under slavery. This is what the nineteenth-century feminist abolitionist Maria W. Stewart said in many of her speeches: "they made bond-men and bond-women of them and their little ones; they have obliged our brethren to labor, kept them in utter ignorance, nourished them in vice, and raised them in degradation."[61] This too was King's critique of white Alabama clergymen who urged civil rights activists to go slow in their agitation against racial segregation:[62] "when your first name becomes 'nigger,' your middle name becomes 'boy' (however old you are) and your last name becomes 'John,' and your wife and mother are never given the respected title 'Mrs.' . . . then you will understand why we find it difficult to wait."[63] Stressing the denial of public political acknowledgment and human dignity and the presumption of black disposability allowed antiracists to expose racism as deeply debilitating in all aspects of human existence. Now white people would have to explain why this was appropriate, necessary, or just. Because many could not, they would lose both the intellectual and moral ground from which to defend it.

Perhaps most crucially, disclosing racism's violent experience was also a pointed way to insist on immediate political

action. Antiracists brought forth what had been authorized
in racism's name: rape, lynching, mutilation, murder, arson,
whippings, beatings, sterilization, scientific experimentation,
solitary confinement, and police brutality. Racism was never
an abstraction for its victims—a matter of intellectual discussion (is it morally right to be a racist?) in the private recesses
of the home or school. This was the point behind Nina Simone's song "Mississippi Goddam" (1964), which said,

> Hound dogs on my trail
> Schoolchildren sitting in jail
> Black cat cross my path
> I think every day's gonna be my last
> . . . .
> I don't trust you anymore
> You keep on saying, "Go slow!"
> "Go slow!"

Racial equality for antiracists meant not simply being
free from the humiliation of sitting in the back of a segregated Birmingham, Alabama, public bus in December
1955—exemplified by the young NAACP secretary Rosa
Parks. Instead it meant not being murdered, like fourteen-
year-old Emmett Till, who was lynched in August of that
year by two white supremacists in Mississippi for glancing
at a white woman, just months before Parks's protest. When
Till's mother, Mamie, insisted on holding an open-casket
funeral so that the world could see how her son was brutalized, she was engaged in an antiracist activity: telling

Americans that her child's disfigured, mutilated face was racism's true face.

Black lived experience of racism thus allowed antiracists to unpack the true meaning of "white privilege." White privilege is not simply the idea that white people can go to well-funded public schools or not be discriminated against in job applications but that they never have to worry about their white skin becoming the object of violence in a society in which black skin conjures those emotional and intellectual associations. Antiracists unmasked euphemisms such as "racial tension," "racial relations," and "racially charged" as deceiving because they hid how racism punished and worked its power on black flesh. In the words of Ta-Nehisi Coates in his memoir *Between the World and Me*, written as a letter to his son in the age of police violence against unarmed black men, "Resent the people trying to entrap your body and it can be destroyed. Turn into a dark stairwell and your body can be destroyed."[64]

Racism's Intersections

Implied in this antiracist perspective shift were myriad experiences of dehumanization. Rarely elaborated by many male antiracists such as King, Douglass, Delany, and Malcolm, this idea was powerfully deepened by black feminist antiracists, who thought the most about the racialized body. Beginning with the educator and activist Anna Julia Cooper in *A Voice from the South*, which argued that the black woman "is confronted by both a woman question and a race problem, and is as yet an unknown or an unacknowledged factor in both,"[65] black feminists drew attention to what the contemporary theorist Patricia Hill Collins called an "interlocking system" of oppression.[66] Feminists both exposed antiracism's blindness to gender and contested universal accounts of oppression. For the contemporary critical race theorist Kimberlé Williams Crenshaw, antiracist avoidance of "intersectionality" made unhearable black women's legal grievances about job discrimination and sexual violence.[67]

Antiracists knew that gendered differences in racist devaluation necessitated different political commitments. Bodily integrity and privacy thus became important sites of struggle. The civil rights activist Fannie Lou Hamer's experience of being raped in a Winona, Mississippi, jail in 1963 for registering rural black Mississippians to vote concretized how patriarchal racism was a form of political suppression. Antiracists politicized black women's private lives and broadened equal citizenship to include possession over one's body and choices over family arrangements. Sojourner Truth said, "I have borne thirteen children, and seen most all sold off to slavery, and when I cried out with my mother's grief, none but Jesus heard me!"[68]

From Racism to Antiracism

Virtually all antiracists believed that abolishing US racial inequality hinged on the white majority moving from nonracism to antiracism.[69] But none believed that white sympathy and rhetorical solidarity were the same as action.

Du Bois's critique of white Republicans abandoning Recon-struction while proclaiming allegiance to ex-enslaved people to secure the presidency in 1877 was extended by Malcolm X when he saw white Democratic politicians in 1963 denounce Jim Crow segregation but do little to solve it: "white liberals are nothing but political hypocrites who use our people as political footballs," he wrote, "only to get bills passed that will increase their own power."[70] Collective inaction in the face of racial domination was not neutral. It has always been easier for those who reap the status quo's benefits to loudly proclaim gradual reform than it is for the dominated to live within it. Understanding this is why everyone from Walker to Delany, Du Bois to Malcolm, preferred the candor of rac-ists to the bad faith of self-proclaimed moderates. As King himself put it, "the Negro's great stumbling block in his stride toward freedom is not the White Citizen's Councilor or the Ku Klux Klanner, but the white moderate, who is more devoted to 'order' than to justice."[71] Antiracists understood that conservatism and racial equality were philosophically at odds. Order placed stability above the uncertainties of freedom. Legality prioritized intact rules over the trans-formative ethical demands of justice. Not doing something terrible is not much better than passively refusing to trans-form society in which many white people benefit and black people suffer.[72]

Many black antiracists were hopeful about white people's embrace of antiracism. But others were not. White supremacy had always been too profitable and persistent in American society. Derrick Bell echoed this Afro-pessimist view shared by some antiracists when he said racism was "an integral, permanent, and indestructible component of this society."[73]

But pessimism never exhausted the antiracist imagination. Few black antiracists could imbibe the blind optimism of their white American counterparts. But none, even the most hopeless, could escape the fact that their demystification of racism—what it was, how it worked, and what it did—was predicated on the possibility of a different future. A fleeting hope that something of the world's beauty was worth fighting for and saving was a staple of antiracism. Of course, political change always hinges on theoretical vision. And nothing concerned antiracists more than developing a political theory of freedom and engaged citizenship. This is the subject to which this book turns next.

3

Fighting for Freedom

Most black antiracists subversively appropriated modern arguments about natural rights that were never extended to them. This is what prompted Frederick Douglass to ask, "Would you have me argue that man is entitled to liberty? . . . You have already declared it."[1] And it prompted James Baldwin to later say that the black person "is not a visitor to the West, but a citizen there."[2] Some antiracists clearly subscribed to the liberal idea of natural equality—that all people are born with inalienable rights—while others had a pragmatic recognition that equality was the dominant language of political claims making. Despite the ideological differences between Martin Luther King Jr. and Malcolm X, for example, King defended political rights, and Malcolm defended human rights. As Malcolm put it, "For me not to have any rights, that's a crime,"[3] and "Twenty million so-called Negroes, second-class citizens, [are] seeking nothing but human dignity and human rights, the right to live in dignity as a human being."[4]

Most antiracists had little patience for arguments that rights were nothing more than empty gestures that only mattered insofar as they are honored by government. To be sure, few thought rights could easily be gained without struggle; but most understood that rights could be used to

oppose racial domination. This is because rights give legitimacy to fundamental, irrevocable guarantees—even if only
symbolically—and express black political equality, from
which more radical arguments about self-determination can
be made.

Rights arguments allowed abolitionists such as Maria
Stewart, Frederick Douglass, and David Walker to say that
the slave system, which stole black people's labor and destroyed their bodies, was inconsistent with the right to life,
free expression, and basic mobility. They allowed T. Thomas
Fortune to say that racial terrorism was inconsistent with the
Fourteenth Amendment's equal protection clause. They allowed Fannie Lou Hamer to say that the sterilization of black
women was inconsistent with the right to privacy. They allowed the Black Panthers in the 1960s to say that police brutality and unjust searches and seizures were inconsistent with
constitutional rights, and they allowed contemporary prison
abolitionists such as Mumia Abu-Jamal to say that mass incarceration was opposed to the protection against cruel and
unusual punishment.

Rights were crucial, but nothing mattered more to antiracists than freedom. "As long as they are human beings," said
Hamer, "they need freedom."[5] Freedom often meant the capacity to make reasonable choices about the good life in ways
unhampered by want or need. From the first ex-slave narratives through today, freedom was connected to autonomy
over one's body and mind. Freedom was about the ability to
engage in self-determination and self-care. But this begged
the questions, How could one determine whether freedom

was in place? What did it mean to be free? What was the barometer by which freedom's realization would be measured?

Most antiracists held that theorizing freedom depended on the perspective of those to whom it was denied, not those who enjoyed it. This was what the jazz singer Nina Simone meant when she sang, "I wish you could know / What it means to be me / Then you'd see and agree / That every man should be free."[6] Listening needed to replace shouting directives from the podium. Understanding specific problems needed to replace simply prescribing answers.

Without question, debates existed in antiracism about whether freedom meant simply the absence of external constraints or the existence of basic resources. Early on, antiracists were more likely to embrace the more "negative" definition, such as that of Douglass, who said, "the freedom from bodily torture and unceasing labor had given my mind an increased sensibility and imparted to it greater security."[7] Later, however, the more capacious version of "freedom to" emerged—as was described in the words of an ex-slave, Paul D, in Toni Morrison's novel *Beloved* (1987): "to get a place where you could love anything you chose—not to need permission for desire—well now, *that* was freedom."[8]

But these theoretical differences were largely about degree and technical definitions. For the vast majority, the black experience of domination led them to have a more expansive view of freedom. Freedom captured a range of experiences and relationships that never really seemed radical to white people: to move along the streets, to eat, to read, to write, to love, and to have friendship and companionship. All are opposed to racism's authoritarian rules and regulations. Hardly any antiracists thus supported a strictly libertarian definition—freedom as narrowly defined by no government intervention into people's lives. Even nineteenth-century conservatives such as Booker T. Washington, black emigrationists such as Martin Delany, and natural-rights-defending liberals such as Douglass, who argued for black self-reliance, never embraced the libertarian philosophical commitment of their white contemporary the social Darwinist William Graham Sumner, who defended a free-for-all fight for limited resources without any guarantee during the Gilded Age, or of some of the most fervent right-wing defenders of abolishing government today.[9]

Support of government efforts aimed at facilitating black equality followed from the antiracist view of freedom. Not being enslaved was not the same as being free. And self-sufficiency was necessary for good choices. This is why Douglass defended a version of self-reliance in the antebellum period but, after the Civil War, defended the federal government's role in providing black citizens economic resources. Douglass proposed a National Land and Loan Company, a government-led initiative that would create a stock company to raise funds to sell or lease land at affordable rates to black freedpeople.[10]

It was impossible to fully separate equal rights from the guarantee of minimal basic resources. Little could come from equal public facilities and public dignity if people were degraded at work or went to crumbling schools. This was A. Philip Randolph's argument in the March on Washington in

1963, which realized his long struggle to gain better working conditions and pay and shorter hours for black workers; he tried to accomplish this through the first black union, the Brotherhood of Sleeping Car Porters, in 1925. As Randolph put it, "we want all public accommodations open to all citizens, but those accommodations will mean little to those who cannot afford to use them."[11]

Though the fact is usually forgotten, Randolph's view was not unlike King's, which itself evolved from calling on congressional leaders to facilitate black voting rights in the early 1960s into a call for interracial economic justice by the end of the decade. On the day he died, on April 4, 1968, King was rallying striking sanitation workers in Memphis, Tennessee, as part of his "Poor People's Campaign." The campaign's "Economic Bill of Rights" was nothing short of radical in its demand for good-paying jobs with a living wage, unemployment benefits, and land access and capital in poor communities.

For all these reasons, monetary reparations for the economic legacy and theft of black labor under slavery and Jim Crow segregation are never far-fetched on antiracist conceptual grounds, even if they have always been viewed as political nonstarters. Reparations were never imagined to be one-time fixed-sum payments per person. From the post–Civil War period, when there was talk of granting black people "forty acres and mule," through today with Movement for Black Lives activists, reparations have usually been linked to creating structural racial equality for the black community. The purpose of reparations, as the SNCC leader James Forman said in his 1969 "Black Manifesto," was to create a land bank for black farmers, a black printing press and media, cultural centers that taught fine arts and liberal studies, welfare programs for needy people, and funds for black workers who partook in labor strikes.[12] More broadly, however, the idea of reparations was a provocation to encourage creative political discussion about American culture. By asking "why not?" antiracists exposed as problematic and modeled an alternative to the idea of narrow self-interest that had long supported racial exploitation and apathy toward black suffering.[13] Reparations countered American individualism and outlined a new version of collective responsibility that was absent in American culture and based in corrective justice—by making whole what was smashed in the past.

Education, Self-Making, and Pluralism

For most antiracists, freedom meant little without a nourished mind. This is why most fought illiteracy and myopic knowledge detached from experience. Nowhere was this goal realized as vividly as in SNCC's Freedom Schools and the Black Panther Party's Liberation Schools in the 1960s. Emphasizing the teaching of black history countered dominant accounts that professed universality but hid partiality. Undercut were narratives of black marginalization that perpetuated racist arguments. Exposed was the social construction and power struggle that defined identity. Antiracists knew that black history had the potential to debunk consensus narratives about US progress and centralize the role of contentious struggle. This still forms one of the best arguments for black studies courses on college campuses—not because they simply enrich US cultural diversity but because they politicize and dismantle romantic images of American identity that remain common sense, not because they reveal black achievements but because they reveal an oppositional set of ideas that transform thinking about society itself.

Freedom Schools and Liberation Schools stressed knowledge based in students' experiences and an open-ended classroom, which modeled an antiracist democratic ethos. Faith in ordinary people to experiment with ideas replaced presumptive suspicions of academic ineptitude.[14] Liberation Schools in particular tried to remake the meaning of community. Focusing on class struggle allowed them to highlight the reasons for black economic exploitation. Connecting students to political prisoners and sponsoring food drives for poor people helped undo the stigmatization and denigration of vulnerable citizens.[15] Here and throughout antiracist thought, education matters because it enables citizens to do what racists say is impossible: to make autonomous decisions, resist strenuous circumstances, and cultivate self-worth. This is why the former SNCC activist and education advocate Bob P. Moses called for education to be a civil right. Moses's "Algebra Project" has trained teachers to improve math literacy for students of color and emphasized the connection between mathematical and political knowledge. Asking deeper fundamental questions about the principles and equations of truth arrived at through deliberation, antiracists believed, is crucial for creating self-governing citizens.[16] Education politicizes people's thinking and is a mechanism through which they can become more engaged. In the words of Kwame Ture, "All real education is political. All politics is not necessarily educational, but good politics always is. You can have no serious organizing without education."[17]

This antiracist defense of education was extended to cultural institutions that cultivated black creativity. No movement defended and realized this goal more vigorously than the 1920s Harlem Renaissance, which created space for black artists to express their sense of complex individuality unconstrained by racial expectations. The dean of the movement, Alain Locke, summarized its philosophical vision of freedom as follows: "The motives of self-expression and spiritual development [will be added] to the old and still unfinished task of making material headway and progress."[18] Cultivating unique black artistic visions expressed the antiracists' thesis that freedom was partly about experimentations with identity that could not be policed. In the Harlem Renaissance, individuality, self-making, cultural creation, social organization, and values and norms were imagined to be unbound. Simultaneously opposed, subverted, and reconstituted were white definitions of conformity, respectability, and propriety.

Many antiracists thus defended the modernist sensibility of "the new." This was captured through what the twentieth-century avant-garde jazz musician Sun Ra called "a different kind of Blackness, the kind / That the world does not know, the kind that the world / Will never understand."[19] It was further visualized through the modernist collage paintings of the twentieth-century painter Romare Bearden, in which found objects were strikingly juxtaposed, layered over, opposed, torn, and stitched to express the ambiguity and multiplicity inherent in, and produced by, free expression and identity, which mirrored the sonic improvisation found in jazz.

Free improvisation was opposed to the rigidity and certainty of racism. An evolving sense of possibility was prioritized over something fixed. This message was often conveyed to citizens of color, but embedded in it was also a lesson for the white majority. Embracing antiracist freedom meant not just supporting black people in their political achievement but renouncing—conscious or unconscious—investments in white supremacy to reconstitute an interracial, improvised democratic future. This was the meaning behind Baldwin's insistence that the white person needed to "be black himself, to be part of that suffering and dancing country that he now watches wistfully."[20]

This antiracist defense of self-expression was based in a respect for a plurality of values. Few antiracists placed this quintessentially liberal idea at the forefront of their political arguments, but many implicitly defended a life uncensored by existing conventions, tastes, and moralities. Even those who were skeptical of this value embodied it. For instance, one of the giants of American literature, the novelist Richard Wright, the author of *Native Son* (1940), thought the Harlem Renaissance was too focused on expressing individuality rather than using art to combat political power. But something of the Renaissance's vision was captured in Wright's argument that artistic social responsibility meant depicting black resistance to capitalism's deprivations. As Wright said, black artists "may say *no* and depict the horrors of capitalism . . . or with hope and passion, say *yes* and depict the faint stirrings of a new and emerging life."[21] Indeed, Wright's creative mode of critique, stemming from his own artistic vision ungoverned by universal expectations, modeled antiracist self-expression. In speaking up against white supremacy and offering a radical vision to counter it, Wright dramatized the view that ideas should be exchanged, debated, and reconstructed rather than sanitized or barred from public discussion on the basis of one's view of the world.

But Wright's anxiety about the apolitical consequences of freedom was also misplaced. Without question, it was impossible to predict what directions freedom would take and realizations it would inspire (for better or worse, whether reasoned or distorted). But rarely would one find naive images of black life in antiracist thought. This was true in the work of figures who were seen to be diametrically opposed. In the 1960s, Amiri Baraka accused Ralph Ellison of being too narrowly obsessed with art for art's sake rather than making art serviceable for radical black politics. But Ellison's great novel *Invisible Man* (1952) painted a harrowing and deeply politicized image of white supremacy denying black individuality. The protagonist's realization that he is "an invisible man . . . [though] no freak of nature, nor history" is developed throughout.[22] The narrative begins with the Battle Royal of black students fighting to the death for limited educational opportunities in the Jim Crow South and unfolds in the urban North in New York, with scenes of housing evictions of poor people and the police killing of an unarmed black man for selling dolls. Likewise, although Baldwin denounced Wright's black protagonist, Bigger Thomas, in *Native Son* as a stereotyped black rapist and murderer, Baldwin admitted that the novel acknowledged precisely what he believed: that black freedom was denied by a long history of racism. Baldwin wrote, "Negroes are Americans. . . . Bigger is their [Americans'] creation."[23]

Dignity, Self-Determination, and Democracy

A pluralistic notion of freedom was the logical extension of the antiracist commitment to equal human dignity. Some antiracists personally and rhetorically expressed commitments opposed to such a pluralistic notion—consider King's homophobia or the black nationalist defense of black patriarchy that can be seen in a range of figures such as Martin Delany and Marcus Garvey. But more often than not, antiracist equality provided the justification for reevaluation and transformation. For instance, Huey Newton rejected his previous homophobia and misogyny and called for making allies with the gay and women's liberation movements. And Amiri Baraka expressed misgivings for his prior anti-Semitic views in a 1980 essay, "Confessions of a Former Anti-Semite," for the *Village Voice*, when he claimed it was "as ugly an idea and as deadly as white racism."[24]

But it was feminists and queer theorists who stressed that antiracist freedom was opposed to exclusionary community values. A vivid example is in Toni Morrison's novel *Paradise* (1997), whose black women of the so-called Covenant—social runaways, castaways, unseen, unheard—counter the patriarchy and rigid moral codes of the male black patriarchs of an all-black town nearby, Ruby, who despise them. *Paradise* defends nonviolent gender nonconformity and bodily sovereignty and opposes violent patriarchal control. Morrison contrasts Ruby, "a backward noplace ruled by men whose power to control was out of control," with the Covenant, which is inhabited by "lively, free, unarmed, females."[25] At stake in *Paradise* is the antiracist reconstruction of normalcy extended to gender. From this perspective, single mothers do not need husbands to thrive. And family could involve the larger community beyond the nuclear household. Freedom comes from women's control over their own bodies, reproductive choices, and sexual desires. This is why Audre Lorde insisted that freedom should be modeled on erotic love. Freedom is about personal liberation through self-awareness: "That self-connection shared is a measure of the joy which I know myself to be capable of feeling, a reminder of my capacity for feeling."[26] Realizing such pleasure and self-care means that exclusionary practices need to go.

Many antiracists believed that no singular way exists to be free. Believing the opposite denies the freedom to determine what relationships are salient and worthwhile and what love and community mean to citizens. And many communities contain histories of repression, violence, and injustice. Antiracists knew not only that exclusion was often done in the name of tradition but that tradition could not recognize that saying no is saying yes to something better. Though Ellison did not identify with black feminism and often was blind to gender, he nonetheless expressed this idea through his critique of the social scientist Gunnar Myrdal's book *An American Dilemma* (1944): "Myrdal sees Negro culture and personality simply as the product of a 'social pathology.' . . . [But] many of the Negro cultural manifestations which he considers merely reflective might also embody a rejection of what he considers 'higher values.'"[27]

Pluralism promoted the idea of self-determination that was central to antiracist thought. The idea that black people should control their own cultural, political, and economic institutions independent of white influence was evident throughout the history of black nationalism with Delany, Garvey, and Malcolm X.[28] And it was expressed through black labor radicalism—socialists, union organizers, communists—who suggested that control needed to exist in the workplace: what collective decisions are made, how labor is organized, and how wealth is disturbed. But no figure so clearly radicalized this antiracist impulse politically than Ella Baker, the radical democratic organizer, former Southern Christian Leadership Council (SCLC) secretary, and chief intellectual inspiration for many students in SNCC in the 1960s. SNCC's activism dramatized the link between democracy and antiracist thought. To be sure, popular rule was not always explicitly defended by antiracists—Du Bois supported a "talented tenth" theory of leadership in which a civic-minded black elite ruled over the masses, and Delany and the early Ida B. Wells and Malcolm X called for leadership by black business leaders.[29] But at some level, many antiracists insisted that popular rule was the extension of equality and agency more than elite rule was. Disagreements with Baker notwithstanding, the Marxist member of the Black Panther Party Fred Hampton, while calling for global anticapitalist revolution in 1969, expressed this idea in the following way: "power to the people!"

"Group-centered leadership" was Baker's theory of organizing that took seriously the local knowledge and experiences of ordinary people in the South. Defending participatory democracy was Baker's critique of King's strategy of hierarchical leadership and charismatic figures. As Baker put it, "I have always felt it was a handicap for oppressed peoples to depend so largely upon a leader, . . . [who] usually becomes a leader because he has found a spot in the public limelight."[30] But also implicit in Baker's and SNCC's activism was that equality was as much a practice as it was a philosophical commitment. Opposition to all forms of hierarchy, on which racist ideas are founded, follows: equality needs to be practiced, assumed, and modeled in everyday life.

By facilitating rather than imposing over student-led organizing (which included many young women, in contrast to King's movement, which was predominantly male led), Baker and SNCC transformed black citizens from passive bystanders into capable political actors. Realized here was the antiracist idea that all citizens are capable of political action and judgment. Urging activists to gather in town-hall settings and allowing for a free-flowing deliberative process in which all perspectives were heard to build consensus undermined arguments about democracy's impracticality. Actualized was the antiracist argument about the importance of respecting difference. Deliberation was transformed into a revelatory exercise, rather than something to be avoided or simply determined in advance.[31]

This is why participatory democracy works for antiracist politics—not because it always successfully achieves policy or legislative objectives but because it counters the democratic despair that power (racist and otherwise) wants. Participatory democracy is further consistent with antiracism because it creates a critical public—of self-sufficient citizens who see community and identity as a work in process, rather than finalized.

As much as antiracists debated ways to achieve freedom, they did not believe it could be achieved through dehumanization. Exceptions existed—some black nationalist emigrationist dreams such as resettlement in Africa implied neocolonialism. But this view was not the rule. Hardly any antiracist arguments defended violence for colonial appropriation and economic exploitation. For some, such as King, a fundamental moral commitment made nonviolence nonnegotiable, while for others, such as Bayard Rustin, violence was strategically counterproductive.

Conversely, antiracist discussions about the ethics of violence revolved around the question of self-preservation in the face of unjust institutions. Nat Turner's nineteenth-century revolt in 1831, which left over fifty people dead, was directed against brutal enslavement; Black Panther arguments for Second Amendment gun rights in the 1960s were mainly about protecting black citizens from the epidemic of police brutality in their neighborhoods. Malcolm X's call for resisting dogs and guns unleashed by Jim Crow segregationists came after witnessing civil rights protestors being beaten on the streets of Birmingham in the summer of 1963. His words captured this pragmatic antiracist sensibility: "Whenever you demonstrate against segregation, whether it is segregated education, segregated housing, or anything else, the law is on your side, and anyone who stands in the way is not the law any longer."[32] Chants of "Freedom Now!" then and now are, for many antiracists, about living without white supremacy, not enriching oneself through what Western democracy was built on: imperialist excursions, global war, slavery, and genocide.

Antiracist Citizenship: Radical Examination and Critique

Antiracist freedom dreams were nothing without reimagined citizenship. Racism depressed black political mobilization as much as it produced a culture of civic respectability. For this reason, no less important in antiracist thought was rethinking basic questions of political life about individualism, responsibility, social relationships, and obligation. Tackling institutions of racial domination required a revolution in the meaning of political action. This began a long process of political engagement—as King put it, "only when the people themselves begin to act are rights on paper given lifeblood."[33]

For many antiracists, critical examination of oneself and one's social reality was a crucial way to undermine the racist epistemological system, which was based in a hierarchical view of human individuality and natural social inequality. Antiracists found little valuable in "conventional wisdom" because exclusionary forces buttressed its common sense. Conventional wisdom insulates one from uncomfortable feelings, troubling thoughts, and unwanted changes. It leaves intact segregated communities, conversations, and thoughts. Intellectual and moral passivity is nothing but a recipe for continued injustice.

Doing the opposite, what King called "the ability to rise to the point of self-criticism," is therefore, as he put it, "one of the sure signs of maturity."[34] Being antiracist involves social critique of fellow citizens. King's call for Christian "agape" to move white self-interest to moral responsibility was perhaps the most famous of such critiques, but his contemporary James Baldwin's was the most unflinching. King modeled compassion to open the black freedom struggle for whites to say all were welcome. As he described it, "*Agape* is disinterested love. It is a love in which the individual seeks not his own good, but the good of his neighbor."[35] But Baldwin announced unpleasant truths about whites' disavowal in an effort to shake them awake from their moral slumber: "Black people are just like everybody else. We are also mercenaries, dictators, murderers, liars. . . . Unless we can establish some kind of dialogue between those people who enjoy the American dream and those people who have not achieved it, we will be in terrible trouble."[36]

The defense of such radical examination stemmed from the view that greater self-knowledge undoes and fractures inherent identities and patterns of thought. Activism could then be bolstered because what emerged was something intellectually deeper and better tested.[37]

Interconnected Struggles and Global Imaginings

Though racism was at the center of antiracists' struggle, they were deeply attuned to related forms of domination. Black socialists, for instance, overturned American individualistic attachment to white skin and antiblack sentiment in favor of understanding shared structural deprivation across race. In the 1910s, Hubert Harrison said, "As long as the workers are despised, the black man will be despised. . . . Socialism is right . . . because any order of things in which those who have the least while those who work them have most is wrong."[38] Today, prison abolitionists associated with the organization Critical Resistance—chanting "Resist!"—try to connect the abolition of racially based mass incarceration with a better-funded health care and educational system for all.[39] Movement for Black Lives activists connect black dignity to gender equality to expose shared social degradation between black citizens, women, queer citizens, and other socially marginalized people. Their platform states,

> We believe in elevating the experiences and leadership of the most marginalized Black people, including but not lim-

ited to those who are women, queer, trans, femmes, gender nonconforming, Muslim, formerly and currently incarcerated, cash poor and working class, disabled, undocumented, and immigrant. We are intentional about amplifying the particular experience of state and gendered violence that Black queer, trans, gender nonconforming, women and intersex people face. There can be no liberation for all Black people if we do not center and fight for those who have been marginalized. It is our hope that by working together to create and amplify a shared agenda, we can continue to move towards a world in which the full humanity and dignity of all people is recognized.[40]

For this reason, many antiracists opposed the idea that they should simply develop narrow political demands. Many knew that segregated progressive visions create segregated movements. Power wants what is connected to appear disconnected. It is much easier for power to tailor opposition to singular movements than to broader ones. This is why antiracists insisted that real political value—rather than moral validation—comes from refreshing and energizing stale political thinking with different perspectives. This is what Audre Lorde had in mind when she said that white feminists ignored black women's struggles against racist patriarchy only to their own detriment: "Only within that interdependency of different strengths, acknowledged and equal, can the power to seek new ways of being in the world generate, as well as the courage and sustenance to act where there are no charters."[41]

From the beginning, being antiracist often meant thinking globally. David Walker's *Appeal* (1829) was a call for solidarity addressed to "Coloured Citizens of the World"; twentieth-century black communists defended working people's struggle worldwide; and antiwar activists defended human rights. Most antiracists viewed narrow nationalist struggles with suspicion. They knew that nationalism refocused attention from global humanity to patriotic identification with US values (capitalism, limited government intervention, and little social welfare benefits) that promoted inequality.

Globalizing antiracism was at the heart of pan-African unity, which was enthusiastically embraced in the 1950s and 1960s during the African independence movements, the rise of the charismatic leader of the Gold Coast Colony (now Ghana), Kwame Nkrumah, and decolonization across the world. Such a global perspective was transformative. For instance, after visiting the African continent in the 1960s, Malcolm X evolved from a defender of capitalism to a proponent of socialism. His support of black entrepreneurship (which he defended during his time with the Nation of Islam) was transformed into a participatory vision of ordinary citizens having control over their lives. Being exposed to shared networks of struggle broadened his understanding of the meaning of community beyond the nation-state toward a fuller idea of the democratic imagination. There was a parallel between Amiri Baraka's argument that "it is necessary to raise the level of our people's political consciousness, so that we are all aware of our commonality and readied to consciously wage a common struggle,"[42] and Malcolm's argument that "our problem is not solved until theirs is solved; . . . theirs is not solved until ours is solved."[43]

A global perspective undid racist myths of deficient US black citizenship and expanded the range of black political futures beyond the US. Black citizens could, on the one hand, see their domination as part of a long European history of exploitation and, on the other hand, imagine as livable places that—from the racist perspective—were imagined as uninhabitable. This idea began with Martin Delany's nineteenth-century black nationalist founding text, *The Condition, Elevation, Emigration and Destiny of the Colored People* (1852), which called for emigration to Central America and Canada. It also later accounted for why both James Baldwin and Richard Wright lived in exile in cosmopolitan postwar Paris in the 1950s and why many black writers and thinkers resettled in Ghana, such as Du Bois, who received Ghanaian citizenship and died there in 1963.

This global perspective also radicalized the meaning of responsibility. Antiracists favored toppling injustice everywhere—boundaries did not matter. Not only was this the logical extension of King's push to nationalize the problem of Jim Crow beyond the South and throughout the US—that "injustice anywhere is a threat to justice everywhere"—but it also explained the political theory behind some antiracist political choices.[44] For example, seeing US economic support of Apartheid motivated Ella Baker to broaden her activism from Jim Crow to South Africa. Malcolm's defense of human rights followed from witnessing the US topple the democratic regime of Patrice Lumumba in Congo. King began to feel solidarity with Vietnamese people being killed by what he called in 1967 the "greatest purveyor of violence in the world today," opposing, and attempting to assume responsibility for, the terrors of American patriotism.[45] Recognizing American imperialistic tendencies throughout the Global South led the cofounder of the Black Panthers Huey Newton to broaden his focus from a US-centric vision of black power to speak about "a revolutionary intercommunalism where [Third World citizens] share the wealth they produce and live in one world."[46]

Fearlessness and Hope

Antiracists transformed fearlessness from a vice into a virtue. In 1828, after Walker's *Appeal* encouraged black citizens to struggle against enslavement by any means necessary, he continued to defend his vision even after a bounty was placed on him, dead or alive. In the 1850s, Douglass addressed sympathetic white audiences even though he was often the only black man in the room. Cooper, Wells, and Lorde were unabashed feminists when doing so brought forth the ire of misogynists across the US. Rustin and Baldwin were both openly gay, when being gay was damaging to their intellectual credibility because of homophobic attitudes in the US.

Being antiracist meant knowing that vulnerability in the face of power was no justification for political quietism. An early critic of Jim Crow, Homer Plessy refused to give up his first-class seat on a Louisiana railroad and became the plaintiff in the US Supreme Court case *Plessy v. Ferguson* (1896), which made constitutional "separate but equal" facilities. Despite the outcome, Plessy's resistance inspired the secretary of an NAACP chapter, Rosa Parks, who refused to sit in the back of a segregated Birmingham bus in 1955. But this antiracist mode of struggle was displayed before both of them, through Ida Wells's full-throated refusal to sit in the back of a segregated railroad car in Memphis in 1883. Confronting power was a way of life for Wells. "I resisted all the time, and never consented to go. My dress was torn in the struggle, one sleeve . . . was almost torn off," Wells said in her testimony. "Everybody in the car seemed to sympathize with the conductor, and were against me."[47] These antiracists prioritized political vision over civility. Freedom was placed above personal peace and civil security. Public action was crucial because it deconstructed political knowledge—who counts, who could be heard, what it means to speak, how to speak, and what claims are legitimate.

Social tension was not entirely without value. Few people now remember that this was exactly what King said was the purpose of the civil rights movement—to use nonviolent direct action "to create such a crisis and establish such creative tension that a community which has constantly refused to negotiate is forced to confront the issue. It seeks so to dramatize the issue that it can no longer be ignored."[48] Recasting exemplary citizenship as defending human dignity provided a standpoint from which to challenge unjust laws. Civil disobedience subverted legally sanctioned inequalities that the majority used to oppress the minority that had no hand in crafting them. This is why King could talk about "unjust laws" and say it was imperative to break unjust laws, "openly, lovingly."[49]

For antiracists, resistance was to be valorized rather than shunned. Radical memories thus needed to be excavated and embraced. Memory expanded antiracist political possibility and challenged the singularity of action. It provided intellectual sustenance to move forward in dark times. This was what Claudette Colvin, who, as a fifteen-year-old in March 1955, refused to sit on a segregated bus nine months before Rosa Parks, said in a later interview: "History had me glued to the seat. Harriet Tubman's hands were pushing down on one shoulder and Sojourner Truth's hand were pushing down on the other shoulder."[50]

Although political realism was crucial for navigating precarious options, antiracists knew that it could become stifling for those who had nothing to gain from what existed. It was better to hope for the impossible to realize the possible. As Harriet Ann Jacobs put it in *Incidents in the Life of a Slave Girl* (1861), "I was dreaming of freedom again; more for my children's sake than my own. I planned and I planned. Obstacles hit against plans. There seemed no way of overcoming them; and yet I hoped."[51] For antiracists, hope meant embracing, rather than withdrawing due to fear of, the unknown. This idea was visualized through the great twentieth-century modernist painter Jacob Lawrence's *Migration Series* (1941), which depicted the Great Migration of black people from the South to the North over the Mason-Dixon line between World Wars I and II. Refugees escaping the landscape of lynching and the strain of poverty allowed Lawrence to depict freedom as something as on the run, ephemeral—there and not there.[52] Forward-looking gazes juxtaposed against the landscape's barrenness visually recast freedom as an entwined relationship between perseverance and the possibility of betrayal, rather than an easily achievable or even totally recognizable ideal. The weight of the luggage positioned against forceful strides staged an idea of freedom as about mobility in the wilderness.

Unfinished Struggle

The tension between freedom's realization and subversion was often preserved in antiracism rather than abandoned, animating broader and more complex dreams to come. For this reason, freedom would always be unfinished. This sensibility, in the words of Angela Davis, that "freedom is a constant struggle"[53] was captured a century earlier by the late nineteenth-century poet Paul Lawrence Dunbar; the poetic speaker of "Sympathy" knew of the caged bird who, though "his wing is bruised and his bosom sore / . . . beats his bars and he would be free / . . . / But a prayer that he sends from his heart's deep core, / But a plea, that upward to Heaven he flings."[54]

Antiracists thus worked through, rather than around, conditions of precariousness. Murder and terror were facts that many black people simply could not escape. The list of the dead is far too long: Thomas Moss, a friend of Ida Wells who was lynched for starting "The People's Grocery," owned by black citizens; the civil rights activist Medgar Evers; Mar-

tin Luther King Jr.; Malcolm X; the Freedom Riders' James
Chaney, Andrew Goodman, and Michael Schwerner; the
Black Panther Fred Hampton; and countless others. But antiracists politicized death and made mourning a site of political
rejuvenation. There was the singing of "We Shall Overcome"
at the conclusion of King's funeral procession and the actor
Ossie Davis's eulogy for Malcolm, which called on future
generations to continue Malcolm's struggle for human rights
and for uniting black people across the globe: "in honoring
him," Davis said, "we honor the best in ourselves."[55] Antiracists recast life as worth living only to the extent that one
was in struggle. Death became an opportunity for reflection.
Reconsolidation and reassessment were placed above retreat.

Expressed here was a melancholic view of action, common
in the black cultural tradition. Black expressions of sorrow
circled and went in the recesses of pain, but rather than facilitate resignation, they transformed persistence into a process
of working through difficult circumstances.[56] Consider the
early slaves' rituals or the "sorrow songs" that introduced the
social criticism of the chapters of Du Bois's *Souls* or the blues
tradition as a whole. This sensibility perhaps was best exemplified through the jazz singer Billie Holiday's song "Strange
Fruit" (1939). Expressing sorrow for lynched black bodies
allowed Holiday to reclaim them. A black future of persistence came from the dead being named, identified, and recognized beyond the violent white landscape in which there
was "blood on the leaves and blood at the root."

Ongoing self-critical engagement was the only way to
combat racism. In the words of A. Philip Randolph, antiracist

freedom struggles required continuous expansion and improvisation into all realms of life: "the struggle must be continuous, for freedom is never a final act, but a continuing, evolving
process to higher and higher levels of human, social, political, economic, and religious relationships."[57] Circumstances
changed, but antiracism always continued. Even if antiracism
arrived late, it never was too late to become antiracist. This is
what Cornel West said after the rebellions in Los Angeles in
1992 after the acquittal of police officers for viciously beating
an unarmed black motorist, Rodney King, an attack that was
recorded and disseminated. "I believe it is late—but maybe
not too late," West wrote, "to confront and overcome the poverty and paranoia, the despair and distrust that haunt us."[58]
"The time is always right to do what is right," King said.[59] One
could not wait, as many white moderates did during King's
time, because, as he wrote, "lukewarm acceptance is much
more bewildering than outright rejection."[60]

Antiracist Engagement

Our contemporary political moment echoes the past. The mix
of nativism, anti-immigrant nationalism, and free-market
deregulation recalls the 1990s' new-right demonization of
free social expression, the attack on the social welfare state,
and the erosion of faith in collective political power. The
antiracist question worth asking today is what Cornel West
asked readers two decades ago: "whether a genuine multiracial democracy can be created and sustained in an era of
global economy and a moment of xenophobic frenzy."[61]

For some people, capacious antiracist freedom dreams seem exceedingly unrealistic or downright utopian, especially when our contemporary moment seems less democratic than ever before with the Trump presidency and the ascendance of right-wing authoritarian regimes across the globe. Discussions of transformative change thus seem misplaced when the public debate is centered on defending basic facts, constitutional liberties, and the post–World War II commitment to human rights—even if only rhetorically and not always substantially. All historical moments suffer from hopelessness. But in every moment, there exist citizens who act without sanction—as if in the dark—to realize a different world. This has been especially true in US history.

Critical pessimism is necessary to frame the contours of realistic limitation and possibility. But dreaming the impossible is equally important. Perhaps the crucial lesson from antiracism is this: all political change begins with dreams, which then become visions that are announced, debated, and fought for in the world. Not all these fights are successful, but some are. Things can change. What once seemed unreal becomes necessary, what was imagined as unacceptable becomes mainstream, what was demonized becomes revered. Antiracist political movements seized the space of the possible and narrowed the meaning of the impossible.

4

Political Movements in Struggle

From the earliest slave rebellions to the contemporary struggle for black equality with the Movement for Black Lives, antiracist movements have been a recurrent presence in US history, mobilizing and inspiring waves of popular energy necessary to confront racism. Their tactics and strategies extracted gains from the political system. Political, social, cultural, and economic conditions shaped their development. But they pushed against what counted as politics, what was acceptable, and what was just. Massive white resistance derailed their aspirations but never entirely and not for too long. Crises forced them to reconsolidate but also provided opportunities for reassessment and renewal.

Antiracist movements answer relevant questions today. What kind of action is politically effective? How should movements organize against political power? What kinds of appeals should they make to citizens? How should they push their agenda? How should they respond to success and failure? How should they balance the goals of resistance and disruption with that of coalition building?

Antislavery and Abolition

The earliest slave activism involved everyday direct action: strikes, rebellions, riots, black women refusing sexual violence, poisonings of slaveholders, sabotage, decreased labor productivity, and feigned ignorance.[1] Slave rebellions provide a counterpoint for those who feel political pessimism today. Ordinary people with no socioeconomic resources were able to provide intense disruption.[2] This is what the pastor and editor Henry Highland Garnet in 1843 declared in the wake of Nate Turner's bloody rebellion in Virginia in 1831 and Denmark Vesey's conspiracy in 1822 to burn Charleston, South Carolina, to the ground: "Brethren, the time has come when you must act for yourselves. It is an old and true saying that, 'if hereditary bondmen would be free, they must themselves strike the blow.'"[3]

Politically, slave rebellions were effective because they put political elites on notice. They issued a challenge to slaveholding Anti-Federalists associated with President Thomas Jefferson in the early 1800s, who mobilized the idea of federalism (the separation of power between state and federal government) found in the Tenth Amendment in the Bill of Rights to argue for states' rights and, thus, slavery. And slave rebellions rejected the false claim by populist Democrats in the 1830s, after the election of President Andrew Jackson in 1828, that equality and freedom had been realized for all given the expanding enfranchisement of the white male electorate. At the same time, however, slave rebellions were effective because they threatened the ways that the slave planation exercised its daily force over and economic exploitation of black people. Success came from attacking the relationships, social dynamics, routines, and schedules that made the planation run smoothly. Serious economic damage was done to slave profit margins. Violence was therefore not the reason for antiracist success—as it created serious blowback that threatened any political gains. Both Nat Turner and Denmark Vesey were hanged, and slaveholders used them as examples to ramp up their racial totalitarian terror. The first antiracist movement was successful because it exploited the very thing slavery relied on: a weak federal government and separation of powers. Certainly, such division codified slaveholder terror and law. But it never facilitated a concerted federal effort that squashed slave rebellions.

Moreover, the antislavery movement's political success hinged on building counternetworks of solidarity that existed underground. Those who think power exists only through controlling the three branches of government are misguided. Antiracists built an invisible counterpublic, which continued the direct action of slave revolts. The Underground Railroad was both a metaphoric and substantive response to the increasing nationalization of slavery.[4] Though it was organized in the late eighteenth century, it reached its peak in the 1850s and 1860s, led by abolitionists such as William Still, Harriett Tubman, and Levi Coffin. Tubman alone helped liberate around two hundred enslaved people, and by some estimates, the Railroad was responsible for bringing tens of thousands above the Mason-Dixon line to the US North and Canada.[5] Informal networks of slaves, free blacks, and white allies created the Railroad's coded language, secret rules, and shifting identities—one was a shopkeeper by day and a freedom fighter by night—and rewrote racial boundaries etched through slavery. Citizens and noncitizens created the community they wished would be realized above ground—which is to say, in public.

This was especially important as slavery became nationalized, first, with the Compromise of 1820, which made Missouri a slave state while making Maine a free one; second, after the passage of the Fugitive Slave Act of 1850, which made runaway slaves in the North subject to retrieval by slave catchers; and third, with what is still called the worst decision in the history of the US Supreme Court, the *Dred Scott* decision (1857), which declared that no black person—whether free or enslaved, who had enslaved ancestors—had legal standing as a citizen.

Nonetheless, antiracists balanced this invisible network with public structured leadership.[6] Antislavery public sentiment was heightened through elite abolitionist figures such as the ex-slave and prolific public speaker Frederick Douglass, the white journalist and publisher of the *Liberator* William Lloyd Garrison, and the black doctor James McCune Smith. And magazines such as David Walker's *Freedom Journal* and Douglass's *North Star* and religious organizations such as the Free Masons and the AME (African Methodist Episcopal) Church were the mechanisms through which ideas about black liberation and white supremacy spread in the public sphere. Moral appeals framed the call for interracial solidarity. Black Christianity became politicized by figurcs such as Walker, Garnet, Maria Stewart, and Douglass. In the words of the black feminist Stewart, "Christ [would have] died in vain . . . unless with united hearts and souls you make some mighty efforts to raise your sons, and daughters from the horrible state of servitude and degradation in which they are placed."[7] Religion became unmoored from scholastic debates about scriptural meaning. Individual moral life was reframed as the radical future hope and justification for ending the evil of slavery. American founding political documents such as the Declaration of Independence and Constitution had a similar function. Douglass, in his famous "What to a Slave Is the Fourth of July?" (1852) recalled the image of revolutionary leadership by identifying himself with the founding generation when he said, "Your fathers, like men of honesty, and men of spirit, earnestly sought redress. They petitioned and remonstrated; they did so in a decorous, respectful, and loyal manner."[8] He retold exemplary citizenship as engaging arbitrary power in all forms—irrespective of race. He recast slaves as the true patriots who, much more so than white Americans, exemplified the revolutionary generation's commitment to liberty.

Although abolitionist patriotic appeals might have been effective, they were not without serious drawbacks. For all their significance, we should remember something that still resonates: imploring black citizens to fight for their dignity can become problematic when it is joined to a moralistic critique of political inaction.[9] Garnet did just this: "But you are a patient people. You act as though, you were made for the special use of these devils. . . . And worse than all, you tamely submit while your lords tear your wives from your embraces and defile them before your eyes. In the name of God, we ask, are you men?"[10] By no means did abolitionists create the "Lost Cause Narrative," but such moralistic narratives nonetheless helped set the rhetorical stage for it after the Civil War; southerners described slavery as a civilizing institution and said it was not that bad—after all, most slaves did not resist all the time. At the same time, patriotic narratives further bolstered hegemonic ideas of American national identity that would eventually be used for imperialist excursions abroad. For instance, Douglass's *North Star* railed against the Mexican-American War in 1846, but arguments about American exceptionalism were used to support the imperialistic annexation of Santo Domingo in 1871, something that Douglass himself supported. This example in particular illuminates the double-edged sword of patriotism for antiracism; it can as much be mobilized against racial injustice as used as justification for racial domination.

Post-Emancipation and Reconstruction

Ultimately, antiracist political struggle evolved after the Civil War from a focus on emancipation to political reconstruction (1863–1877). Former abolitionist claims about slavery's brutality were transformed into "radical" Republican arguments about the necessary resources for equal citizenship.

Even though radicals were not always successful, they pushed Republican presidents such as Abraham Lincoln and then Andrew Johnson to reject leniency for the South after the

Civil War. This was one way they capitalized on the fracturing of traditional political solidarities and the collapse of the slave-holder economy. Radical Republicans thus provide contemporary lessons for making freedom claims in times of crisis. With tremendous speed, they unapologetically pushed their freedom demands. The Thirteenth Amendment to the US Constitution, which outlawed slavery, was passed in the House and Senate before the end of the war, while the Fourteenth, which granted black citizens equal treatment under the law, and the Fifteenth, which gave them the right to vote, both came in 1868. Much in the same way that abolitionists' calls to end slavery expanded the meaning of what was possible, some radicals called for the redistribution of rebel lands to ex-slaves and, when this plan was abandoned, defended the Freedmen's Bureau, a federal agency formed in the Department of War that was designed to facilitate black uplift through economic resources, education opportunities, shelter, and food.[11] Though Douglass's firm commitment to private property prevented him from defending the redistribution of land, he nonetheless petitioned Congress to support the Freedmen's Savings and Trust Company, created in 1865 to grant black people affordable loans to start anew—he was appointed its president in 1874.[12]

But Douglass himself was part of the first formal black political class in the US, which was expressed through recently elected black representatives throughout the South in the Republican Party. A unique opportunity was created here for black control and self-governance. Black-led community organizations flourished, education increased, and voting rates spiked dramatically.

Nonetheless, what Du Bois thought was the first genuinely multiracial experiment in democracy was defeated
because of its own success.[13] The massive number of newly
enfranchised black citizens were met with a violent backlash
of "night riders" associated with the KKK. These white supremacists had as their sole purpose enforcing black political inaction through violence and intimidation. And white
Republican politicians did not help. To the contrary, the infamous Tilden-Hayes compromise of 1877 concluded a bit-
terly contested election of 1866 that ended in a discrepancy
between the Electoral College vote and the popular vote.
Republican Rutherford B. Hayes lost the popular vote to
Democrat Samuel Tilden, but twenty electoral votes—from
Louisiana, South Carolina, Florida, and Oregon—remained
disputed, as each party claimed its candidate had won them.
The issue was resolved after an informal agreement in which
Hayes gained the presidency with the concession to Democrats that he would withdraw federal troops that, as part
of Reconstruction, enforced black political equality in the
South. Shorty thereafter, the Jim Crow regime of racial segregation arrived, and black politics was resolutely repressed,
especially after the *Plessy* decision of 1896 codified the constitutional legitimacy of "separate but equal" public spaces.
What had been almost full black male political participation
plummeted to less than 5 percent at the end of the century.[14]

Resisting Jim Crow

A new set of problems confronted antiracists. How could they fight white supremacy when it had not only proven so durable but also, after *Plessy*, successfully adopted the rhetoric of social equality to actualize its goals? Antiracists had their work cut out for them not only because black liberation seemed like an afterthought after the massive inequality created through the Gilded Age but also because government nonintervention began to be justified as the new public philosophy.

Antiracists adopted a new strategy. Two camps defined the new generation of leaders pushing for racial uplift of the black masses. On the one hand, there was Booker T. Washington's position of racial accommodation, which extended Douglass's pre–Civil War thinking about black self-reliance. Washington's gamble was that black uplift would best be accomplished through black citizens' mutual cooperation with white elites and cultivation of industrial skills for economic improvement and social advancement. This is what Washington meant by his famous declaration in 1895 in his Atlanta Exposition Address to black southerners, "cast down your bucket where you are"—that happiness would "proceed from the possession of property, of intelligence, and high character."[15]

Abandoning political agitation may have bolstered Washington's status as a respected figure, but it did little to build a mass movement capable of confronting Jim Crow. Calling for black citizens to embody industriousness comported with the demands of late nineteenth-century capitalism, but it did not tackle the chain gangs and sharecropping that were the expression of black socioeconomic domination or the precarious existence of black life because of lynching.[16]

In contrast, the more politically successful movement, which sought to tackle these problems, was the National Association for the Advancement of Colored People (NAACP), which was founded in 1909 by, among others, W. E. B. Du Bois. Though Du Bois was criticized for subscribing to the notion that "the talented tenth" of elites was the essential class for leadership, he never abandoned direct action and political agitation to make life better for the black majority.[17]

For Washington, uplift became a way to pragmatically acquire respectability in the white mainstream. But for Du Bois and the NAACP, political agitation for equality became a way to capitalize on and connect with the burgeoning progressive movement of the early twentieth century, which sought to abolish what the Gilded Age produced: disastrous labor conditions for workers, unchecked child labor, public health crises, and stifling poverty. To be sure, many white progressives at the time made little mention of racism. But the NAACP nonetheless linked its struggle to their liberal reformist vision and, after World War I, to the democratic values of American nationalism. Lobbying and legal challenges in the courts became the primary ways for the NAACP to be heard. The petition, oral argument, and legal test case became tools through which the organization radicalized the American rhetoric of equality. The NAACP was thus an extension of earlier, critical antiracist counterpublics: it had the spirit of abolitionist activism and made its claims to political elites, but unlike black politicians during Reconstruction, it was not formally institutionalized in the political sphere.

The NAACP was at its core a tool for public persuasion.[18] And nothing preoccupied it more than the national campaign against lynching. Ironically, those who led the antilynching struggle were only tangentially associated with the NAACP because they thought it was too moderate: T. Thomas Fortune, who was the founder of the radical National Afro-American League and the editor of the *New York Globe*, and the journalist-activist Ida B. Wells. Like abolitionists before them, both figures demonstrated the political power of the pen. Fortune would sometimes rely on constitutional arguments, while Wells appealed to Americans' sense of the rule of law. To be sure, such patriotic appeals threatened to cement the hegemonic exceptionalist narrative used to justify late nineteenth-century US racist imperial expansion and war abroad.[19] But both Fortune and Wells pushed the boundaries of political claims making. For example, the argument for shared interracial economic interest was woven throughout Fortune's early Marxist work *Black and White: Land, Labor and Capital in the South* (1883), which held that white racism and violence shielded white workers from recognizing that "*the condition of the black and the white laborer is the same, and . . . their cause is common*; that they should unite under the one banner and work upon the same platform of principles for the uplifting of labor, the more equal distribution of the products of labor and capital."[20] Wells, unlike Fortune, who influenced her, recast the meaning of citizenship to include the perspective of women and to make gender essential in political struggle. Highlighting the idea of white chivalry as a bogus justification for lynching allowed Wells to represent women as capable agents and to show how gender could be weaponized for murder.[21] On the one hand, chivalry was not the true cause of lynching because, as she outlined in *A Red Record* (1894), people were lynched for a wide range of reasons, many of them trivial—such as fraud, insults, vagrancy, and often for no stated reason at all. On the other hand, in *Southern Horrors* (1892), Wells rejected the fantasy that white women were victims of black male aggression. To the contrary, they were often the initiators of consensual interracial relationships: "Afro-American men do not always rape white women without their consent. . . . White men lynch the offending Afro American, not because he is a despoiler of virtue, but because he succumbs to the smiles of white women."[22]

More broadly, however, the antilynching movement sought to engage America's conscience by playing on lynching's macabre visual culture of photographs and postcards. In this respect, the brutalized black body was represented as a test case for American democracy when this commitment was being defended during World War I and in its aftermath by the Democratic president Woodrow Wilson's "Fourteen Points" plan, which called for liberal internationalism and worldwide peace. The movement depicted lynching's brutality as the logical conclusion of the new racist ideology being born through the resurgence of social Darwinism and the eugenics movement—as well as the racist cultural image of deviant black male sexuality perpetuated by films such as D. W. Griffith's *The Birth of a Nation* (1915), which Wilson himself screened at the White House and called a great film. Nonetheless, the antilynching movement did not stop at arguments or rhetoric aimed at public consciousness-raising or persuasion. It always connected its campaign to the objective of black political enfranchisement. Federal laws banning lynching, rather than leaving it up to states and localities that always exonerated lynch mobs, were seen as the only real corrective.

Black Labor Radicalism

Political success was elusive. No major legislative gains could be celebrated from the 1890s through the 1930s—when over three thousand people were lynched. But what Wells called a bloody "red record" gave way to the "red fever" of black labor radicalism, which encompassed the radical labor, communist, and socialist movements. Black economic radicalism in the US generally emerged after the Bolshevik Revolution of 1917 in Russia inspired subjugated people across the world. Given the historical moment, black enthusiasm for working-class power made sense. Growing economic insecurity in the US was spurred by reckless, unregulated capitalism during the Roaring Twenties of wealth and luxury for the upper classes and justified through the Republican president Herbert Hoover's philosophy of "rugged individualism." This created both the Great Depression and the very class of dispossessed white and black workers who were both capitalism's biggest victims and greatest source of opposition.[23]

Many black labor radicals never explicitly identified with antilynching activists and sometimes gave them a cold shoulder. But the labor radicals' strategies resonated with the antilynching activists through an appeal to shared economic interests across the racial line. An example of this was the Southern Tenant Farmers' Union (STFU), which was called into being by the Socialist Party leader Norman Thomas and was organized in 1934 by sharecroppers in Arkansas who did not receive a fair share of a New Deal subsidy program given to landowners for whom they worked.[24]

As for earlier antiracists, organization was crucial for these radicals, especially when racism was so widespread within the predominantly white national labor movement and unregulated capitalism was such a powerful force. But their focus departed from earlier struggles. They were not elite led or middle class centered. Instead, the black working class was both its leadership and focus. The first black labor union—the Brotherhood of Sleeping Car Porters in 1925, led by the socialist A. Philip Randolph—struggled for black workers' rights, a shorter work week, greater job security, and better pay. But much more crucial, and politically effective, was its mode of direct action. The first black NAACP secretary, James Weldon Johnson, went so far as to say that the general strike was "the mightiest weapon in the hands of the colored people."[25] To be sure, strikes, like earlier slave rebellions, were squashed with brutal state violence that exceeded that in other countries; and they were incredibly risky precisely because the threat of replacement labor was always lurking around the corner. But the increasing size and power of the black working class, which was entwined with the rapid growth of the US industrial sector, made strikes a powerful tool for gaining concessions from the interests of capital. They transformed black economic vulnerability into a form of power.

At the same time, labor radicals knew that context mattered. In the North, the short-lived communist African Blood Brotherhood (ABB), led by Cyril Briggs from 1919 to 1921, fused Marcus Garvey's black nationalism with pan-African solidarity—which was gaining widespread influence throughout the 1920s. The ABB resonated with the black urban population toiling under brutal factory conditions, in which free labor was assumed but nonetheless exploited.[26] In the Jim Crow South, however, black communists such as Hosea Hudson joined the objective of black political rights to economic freedom in order to challenge the regime of racial authoritarianism. Hudson knew that audience mattered: black southern sharecroppers, who were deeply religious, needed to be moved in ways that stressed their faith rather than Marxist class analysis and theories of historical materialism.[27]

Black labor radicals, as antiracists before them, pushed the boundaries of democratic New Deal liberalism led by Franklin Roosevelt. The New Deal claimed to make good on the promise of progressivism in theory, but—given that the racist "Solid South" was a key part of its coalition and that state-directed initiatives were a way through which resources were distributed—actually excluded black people in practice. Local labor struggles politicized black citizens in ways that gave them voice and made racial justice a centerpiece of economic justice—a position that up until then it had never been given. In broadening equality to mean workers' rights, they further expanded the meaning of freedom, from something that could be realized through a compassionate regulatory state to one that supported black autonomy.

But much like during Reconstruction, antiracist economic radicalism was threatened by the organizations and interracial coalitions that initially made it successful. A tepid response from the American Federation of Labor (AFL) led the Brotherhood of Sleeping Porters to lose political momentum. The top-down directives from the Soviet Union led the US Communist Party (CP) to betray the interest of racial equality, even though after its legal defense of the "Scottsboro Boys" in 1931—which saw nine young black men wrongfully accused of raping two white women—it became a prominent force with many black intellectuals and workers in ways unmatched by the NAACP. Nonetheless, the CP's embrace of patriotism at the expense of racial equality led writers such as Richard Wright to defect from the party in 1942. The CP called for black members to support US involvement in World War II without acknowledging how the army was racially segregated and that black citizens had little reason to fight for a country that dehumanized them. Wright understood that patriotism could easily be used to distract from the antiracist freedom struggle at home and serve as a blank check for the US military apparatus abroad.[28] The other main reason radicals lost momentum was that the antipathy between various ideological factions—communists, socialists, and liberals—was as threatening for solidarity as the violence unleashed by big business to thwart radical dissent.

The Long Civil Rights Movement

Black labor radicalism left a mark less through its concrete legislative gains and more through what it inspired in the civil rights movement of the 1950s and 1960s. Activists such as Randolph—who was, tellingly, one of the keynote speakers at the 1963 March on Washington for Jobs and Freedom— finally took its ideas to a national audience. The civil rights movement was also a culmination of twenty years of black political activity—after black World War II veterans in the postwar period who fought fascism abroad in the name of democracy returned home to segregation.

Undeniably, the civil rights movement formed the apogee of antiracist struggle in the US. It was, as some people have aptly called it, the "second reconstruction."[29] It had four main ideological factions—black nonviolent integration led by King and Bayard Rustin and the SCLC; black nationalism led by Malcolm X; Marxist-oriented and internationalist-focused black power led by young radicals such as Stokely Carmichael, Huey Newton, and Elaine Brown in urban black areas; and popular democratic struggles in the rural South led by Ella Baker and the students associated with SNCC. Each had different tactics, but together they responded to the postwar moment.[30] New political coalitions formed and pragmatic strategy shifts materialized precisely as old regimes such as the New Deal political coalition were crumbling, new social liberation movements especially in the late to mid-1960s were forming, and the meaning of black equality was changing at breakneck speed.[31]

King and the SCLC

In what has come to be known as the "mainstream" integrationist wing of the civil rights movement (CRM), activists such as King and the SCLC followed a long antiracist tradition to exploit new political opportunities and bolster their claims. The 1954 U.S. Supreme Court decision *Brown v. Board of Education*, which made public school segregation in the South unconstitutional, was the precursor of the Montgomery Bus Boycott in 1955. The boycott was inspired by Rosa Parks's refusal to give up her seat on a segregated bus and lasted 381 days. Rather than take the bus, black boycotters used other means of transportation—they would walk, bike, or carpool. Soon, an informal network began to spring up to sustain them: black churches collected money to purchase better shoes for pedestrian boycotters; black taxi drivers began charging the bus fare as a flat rate. The boycott not only had a profound economic impact on the city of Montgomery but began a decade of nonviolent direct actions that culminated in the passage of civil rights legislation in the 1960s.

Rhetorically, the integrationist wing of the CRM used patriotism to make its arguments about racial justice. King's invocation of the Declaration of Independence was about pushing America to realize at home what had been its geopolitical concern abroad—as the moral alternative to Soviet communism, which was being embraced by revolutions across the globe by people of color in Africa and Central America.[32] As King put it in his famous "I Have a Dream" speech on August 28, 1963,

> Five score years ago, a great American, in whose symbolic shadow we stand signed the Emancipation Proclamation. . . . But one hundred years later, we must face the tragic fact that the Negro is still not free. One hundred years later, the life of the Negro is still sadly crippled by the manacles of segregation and the chains of discrimination. One hundred years later, the Negro lives on a lonely island of poverty in the midst of a vast ocean of material prosperity. One hundred years later, the Negro is still languishing in the corners of American society and finds himself an exile in his own land. In a sense we have come to our nation's capital to cash a check. When the architects of our republic wrote the magnificent words of the Constitution and the Declaration of Independence, they were signing a promissory note to which every American was to fall heir. This note was a promise that all men would be guaranteed the inalienable rights of life, liberty, and the pursuit of happiness.[33]

Throughout US history, racist brutality had been done out of sight, in secret, and out of mind—in the planation, the bedroom, the field, and in the dark of the night. But King repurposed the violence written on the black body. The violated, lifeless black body that antilynching activists

presented to outrage American conscience became transformed into a freedom-desiring citizen. Protests and sit-ins,
which exhibited well-groomed and well-dressed young
activists, visualized the idea that racial segregation was
an opposition between righteous moral Christians who
endured the humiliation, body blows, water hoses, and
attack dogs and the hateful immoral racists who were violent without compunction or any serious thought. Think of
the Freedom Rides, the freedom marches, the Selma march,
the Birmingham march, and the mass demonstrations of
interlocking arms. Antiracist, nonviolent action created
an image of black protest that became less threatening to
whites. Sympathetic white liberals could therefore accept
the movement.[34]

Such public performance at its heart exposed the ironies
of democratic membership. Antiracists staged their opposition to the rage and thoughtlessness consuming white onlookers, who only gained something by not losing their false
sense of white supremacy. This juxtaposition was most powerfully captured through the photograph of Elizabeth Eck-
ford, who was spat on and verbally assaulted as she walked to
class to desegregate Little Rock High School in 1957, as well as
through the 1960 Greensboro, North Carolina, sit-ins, where
protestors sat on lunch counters as food was poured on their
heads. In an age when a new form of media—television—
could make these narratives visible in every home across the
nation, activists had the unique advantage of information
dissemination that exceeded just about every other antiracist
movement that preceded them.[35]

As much as such presentations of black respectability were crucial for the movement, they nonetheless distracted public attention from the direct assault on power. Nonviolence was morally nonnegotiable, but its impact was every bit as radical as earlier slave rebellions and labor strikes. Sit-ins disrupted the flow of business, while boycotts shut down the southern economy, which absolutely depended on low-wage black labor. Marches blocked automobile traffic and, consequently, the timely and efficient distribution of goods across the country. Though the movement directed its demands toward established forces of power, it also placed tremendous pressure on them. By dominating the headlines and forcing the Democratic administrations of John F. Kennedy and then Lyndon Johnson to choose between the black electorate whom they claimed to represent and the southern whites who were still part of their electoral coalition, the movement exploited various political divisions to its advantage.

It is true that the movement's top-down, male-led strategy of leadership threatened to derail its liberatory aspirations and alienated a whole generation of young people who gravitated toward more radical options. But like earlier antiracists, the SCLC maintained pragmatic flexibility and was responsive to changing realities. Though the commitment to nonviolence remained, the SCLC rethought its agenda to emphasize democratic socialism and broadened its coalition to include workers and antiwar activists struggling against the Vietnam War and US imperialism abroad. Growing disenchantment about Democratic politicians' commitment to black socioeconomic equality even after the Civil Rights Act of 1964 outlawed legal discrimination and Voting Rights Act of 1965 guaranteed equal voting rights led King to commit himself to a "Poor People's Campaign" of interracial economic justice, just months before he was assassinated.[36]

SNCC

One of King's greatest contributions was to open a political space through which to normalize discussions of black liberation and expand them more profoundly. It was this space that was seized by SNCC in 1963 and 1964 throughout its campaign in rural Mississippi, which was the poorest and most violent of the Jim Crow states. SNCC shared SCLC's integrationist vision, but—following earlier labor activists and communists—took the energy, knowledge, and commitments of local communities as the starting point for organized collective action. In this way, it was more willing to break rules than SCLC was. Moral appeals and shared interest were less important for SNCC than direct political action was. Moreover, unlike SCLC, SNCC's success came from its decentralization, which created networks of resistance, whose autonomy and dispersion worked to counter the localized structures of domination, with all their intricacies and hidden crevices. As Ella Baker put it,

> The Student Leadership Conference made it crystal clear that current sit-ins and other demonstrations are concerned with something much bigger than a hamburger or even a giant-sized Coke. . . . The students showed willingness to be met

on the basis of equality, but were intolerant of anything that smacked of manipulation or domination. This inclination toward *group-centered leadership*, rather than toward a *leader-centered group pattern of organization*, was refreshing indeed to those of the older group who bear the scars of the battle, the frustrations and the disillusionment that come when the prophetic leader turns out to have heavy feet of clay.[37]

SNCC thus provided an exemplary model, like labor activism before it, for giving citizens political efficacy to exercise their collective political power and democratic deliberation skills. This occurred primarily through town-hall-style discussions that would end when there was a general consensus reached, and citizens were encouraged to speak as long as they wished.[38]

But over time, SNCC eventually shifted gears, even going so far as to deemphasize its absolutist commitment to nonviolence by changing its name to the Student *National* Coordinating Committee in 1969. Increased police brutality, decrepit living conditions for the urban black poor, and a feeling of hopelessness especially after the Watts rebellion of 1965 (a black uprising lasting two weeks, triggered after a police officer pulled over and fought a black motorist) led SNCC and its new militant leader, Stokely Carmichael, to shift course. As Carmichael put it in Berkeley, California, in 1966, "We gonna use the word 'Black Power' and let them address themselves to that; (*applause*) but that we are not goin' to wait for white people to sanction Black Power. We are tired of waiting; every time black people move in this country, they're forced to defend their position before they move. It's time that the [white] people who are supposed to be defending their position do that. . . . They ought to start defending themselves as to why they have oppressed and exploited us."[39] Under Carmichael's leadership, SNCC transformed from an organization advocating integrationist pacifism to one of black power through any means necessary and aligned with the radical white student organization Students for a Democratic Society (SDS) in its antiwar stance against the Vietnam War.[40]

Black Nationalism

Black nationalism in the 1950s and early 1960s was a countervision to civil rights integration and SNCC participatory democracy.[41] Organizations such as the Nation of Islam (NOI), led by Elijah Muhammad, whose most famous spokesperson was once Malcolm X, appealed directly to black citizens. On some level, the NOI extended antiracist attempts at cultivating black solidarity in the civic sphere to oppose white supremacy by establishing alternative black civic spaces, by politicizing Islam, and by supporting black business. But the NOI's narrow appeal to black citizens accounted for its biggest difference from most politically successful antiracist movements, which engaged across the racial line. And the NOI's explicitly capitalist, entrepreneurial economic vision—like Booker T. Washington's self-reliance philosophy and Marcus Garvey's Universal Negro Improvement

Association (UNIA)—was counterproductive to the economic interests of the black working-class majority.[42]

Both of these elements accounted for Malcolm's break with the NOI in 1964. Malcolm began to develop his own voice. King's patriotism and morality were rejected in Malcolm's speeches and were replaced with arguments about black-led but democratically accountable political, cultural, and economic institutions. As Malcolm put it, "We want justice by any means necessary. We want equality by any means necessary. . . . We don't think that we should have to sit around and wait for some segregationist congressmen and senators and a President from Texas in Washington, D.C., to make up their minds that our people are due now some degree of civil rights."[43] Unlike King, Malcolm's pessimism toward engaging American political elites remained throughout, but— especially in the last year of his life—it did not preclude him from calling on white allies to join the struggle. Malcolm's rage at white supremacy was real, but it never made him enact violence toward his political enemies, even though he was eventually assassinated by one of them—a NOI member. The organization Malcolm developed in his final year, Organization of Afro American Unity (OAAU), failed to realize his goal of developing black-led institutions that competed with the NOI. But it maintained what was a hallmark of successful antiracist politics: a broad commitment to global human rights, interconnected struggle, and the preservation of black dignity through concrete economic resources rather than merely political rights.[44]

The Black Panthers

In the final analysis, Malcolm's political life was ultimately not as long as his shadow on the future. He was more a philosopher and public leader than an organizer or professional activist. He did not inspire the same kind of seismic political shifts as King and the SCLC did, but importantly, he energized young black radicals to live a life of radical engagement. Indeed, few organizations crystallized Malcolm's final vision as much as the Black Panther Party for Self-Defense. What united both it and early SNCC—the organization from which many of the Black Panthers' later members came after 1967—revealed crucial lessons for antiracist activism. Respectability is not the only way to make claims. Extensive organizational resources are not always essential. Life experience does not necessarily trump youthful exuberance. Shared political and socioeconomic interests could be directed toward black citizens, rather than white ones.

The Panthers were founded by the young black radicals Huey P. Newton and Bobby Seale in Oakland, California, in 1966, as a response to police brutality and urban economic deprivation. The Panthers fashioned themselves as a left-wing paramilitary organization and blended Malcolm's idea of black power, the rhetoric of American patriotism (they defended the Second Amendment's right to bear arms), and "Third World" radicalism—the teachings of Mao Zedong and Che Guevara.[45] The Panthers, and especially Newton, were rightly criticized for their misogyny. But their one-time chairperson from 1974 to 1977, the black feminist Elaine

Brown, summarized the philosophy as follows: "Each time, each place, the people will take the lead from us, the revolutionary vanguard. Just as the people have institutionalized our Free Breakfast for Children and sickle-cell anemia programs, they will demand socialized medicine and decent housing. . . . [Then] the black people and poor white people and oppressed people all over America, will rise up like a mighty tide and wash clean this beachfront of capitalism and racism, and make the revolution!"[46]

One famous example of Panther politics was when members descended on the California State Assembly in 1967 to protest the legislature's attempt to ban the public carrying of firearms. This served to dramatize the value of black life, but it was ultimately less effective than the community programs that the Panthers established (schools, breakfast programs for kids, shelter, small loans, buses to prisons, mental health treatment facilities), which, like SNCC, pushed the boundaries of participatory democracy. Contrary to popular misconceptions of Panther ideological absolutism, the organization's political strategy was pragmatic. Attempts were made to broaden political coalitions away from primarily black organizations to, as Newton put it, "full participation of the gay liberation movement and the women's liberation movement."[47]

The image of the Panthers walking with guns and berets had a negative impact on their public reception, which diminished their reach. Potential allies rejected what they saw as the Panthers' apolitical radical chic (that the movement was more about the aesthetics of resistance than the real thing), while others denounced what they perceived to be a fearsome blackness. But Panther activities contributed to the militant atmosphere evident in the black rebellions in Watts, Newark, and Detroit, which led to the famous Kerner Commission of 1967, established by President Johnson, to declare the necessity of "a comprehensive and enforceable federal open housing law."[48] Partly because of the Panthers' efforts, within a week of King's death on April 4, 1968, Congress passed what was generally seen as one of the most important socioeconomic pieces of civil rights legislation, the Fair Housing Act, which legally ended housing discrimination and the practice of redlining.

Reaction and Backlash

These four divergent antiracist movements responded to different problems, populations, and political circumstances. But by the end of the 1960s, they dissipated. Certainly internal divisions, political choices, and loss of leaders played a role: Malcolm was assassinated in 1965; King was assassinated in 1968; the Chicago Panther Fred Hampton was killed in a police raid in 1969; Huey Newton was jailed in 1968; and the former Panther Angela Davis was jailed in 1970. And SNCC, led by Carmichael, became less effective. But the fundamental issue was never the movements themselves but concerted state repression. Recall that then-director of the FBI J. Edgar Hoover once called King the most dangerous man in America and led an effort to sow divisions within the Panthers.

Moreover, as with the first Reconstruction, popular white backlash emerged on the scene immediately at the onset of the second. Massive resistance against school desegregation in the 1950s culminated in the election of the Republican Richard Nixon in 1968. He successfully brought into the Republican coalition the white electorate that felt deep racial resentment after the passage of the 1960s civil rights bills. This was the electorate that Johnson himself believed was lost for Democrats nationally. And it was the electorate in both the North and the South that the segregationist Alabama governor George Wallace—who proudly proclaimed in 1963, "segregation now, segregation tomorrow, segregation forever"—spoke to in his 1968 bid for president.

Wallace lost, but Nixon built his "law and order" platform by playing on white fears of black extremism and militancy. Black militancy became a wedge for Republicans through which to distract citizens from the global, interconnected, and socioeconomically focused form that antiracism was beginning to take in the late 1960s. Just like a century earlier, hope of black liberation was faced with the stark reality of its reversal. By the late 1970s, the retreat from equality was already in full swing—the Supreme Court chipped away at mandated-busing programs with its *Milliken v. Bradley* (1974) decision, which derailed efforts at public school integration. Moreover, overturned through popular referendum and ballot initiatives in various states were affirmative-action programs meant to bring black people onto an equal playing field after centuries of white supremacy. Many white Ameri-

cans even began invoking the language of "reverse discrimination," which held that white people were the true victims
of corrective justice measures. For all of these reasons, the
antiracist struggle in the post-civil-rights era by the early
1980s became about not expanding black freedom dreams
but simply maintaining what was gained in the 1960s.[49] This
was expressed through the transformation of former student
activists such as John Lewis, who was elected as a Democratic congressman from Georgia in 1987, and Jesse Jackson,
who unsuccessfully sought the Democratic Party presidential nomination for president in 1984 and 1988, into political elites working from within the reformist parameters of
American liberalism.

And even this was no easy task. A conservative political
climate, which was compounded by the Republican assault
on the social welfare state during the Ronald Reagan presidency (1980–1988), helped depress the spirit of black protest.
Antiracist ideas suffered another serious blow through the
rise of black conservative public intellectuals such as Shelby
Steele, John McWhorter, and Thomas Sowell, who, by the late
1980s and early 1990s, dominated the mainstream and gained
visibility through nationally syndicated media, magazines,
and newspapers. Echoing Booker T. Washington's argument
about black self-help and preaching "color-blind" policies,
they called for minimal government intervention that only
perpetuated systemic racial inequality.

Black freedom dreams thus burned to ash, and the clarity
of antiracist voices was obscured. This was metaphorically
dramatized in the powerful conclusion of Spike Lee's *Do the*

Right Thing (1989), in which the penultimate scene shows Smiley—a figure who has a pronounced stammer—placing an image of the iconic photograph of King and Malcolm's only meeting, on March 26, 1964, onto the burning rubble of Sal's Pizzeria as it is being burned down by black citizens after one of their own, Radio Raheem, has been strangled to death by a white police officer.

Antiracism in the Post-Civil-Rights Era

Not all antiracist energy was lost after the 1960s. Much of it took a new form. The black public sphere, which had earlier circulated through historically black colleges and black newspapers such as the *Pittsburgh Courier* and journals such as *Crisis*, became active through curriculums across college campuses from the 1980s onward.[50] The creation of this new antiracist culture and civil sphere was made possible through King's mainstreaming of justice talk. But it was much more influenced by late-1960s black radicalism. Antiracist academics coming of age then tried to revive what seemed lost in the prior decades. The first black studies program was founded at San Francisco State University in 1968, but by the 1980s, many were in existence in universities across the US. Black studies emphasized the teaching of black history, marginalized black voices, and counterpatriotic narratives that challenged consensus narratives of American history. Black studies for "Afrocentrists" such as Molefi Kete Asante became a way to challenge Eurocentrism (which privileged the philosophy and values of western European peoples) and the modern political ideas it engendered. For Afrocentrists, embodied thinking drawn from the African experience and philosophy and culture were prioritized over western European universality, social consciousness over individualism, and historicity over the inevitability of progress.[51]

A new generation of black feminists and queer activists also had a profound effect on women's and gender studies academic departments. What was hailed as an intellectual breakthrough in both the women's and black liberation movements, the Combahee River Collective statement in 1974, written by black lesbian activists who met in Cambridge, Massachusetts, argued that political action required understanding and responding to the interlocking nature of oppression on the basis of sex, class, gender, and race that many women of color faced. As the collective put it, "The most general statement of our politics at the present time would be that we are actively committed to struggling against racial, sexual, heterosexual, and class oppression, and see as our particular task the development of integrated analysis and practice based upon the fact that the major systems of oppression are interlocking."[52] Black feminists transformed lived experience into a source of theory, they used black women's voices to disrupt male-saturated fields of thinking, and they linked gender to racism and capitalism in explaining US patriarchy.[53] In the words of bell hooks, "The struggle to end racism and the struggle to end sexism are naturally intertwined. . . . To make them separate [is] to deny a basic truth of our existence, that race and sex are both immutable aspects of human identity."[54] For black feminists, to think in interconnected ways required undoing false binaries and hierarchies of oppression. Doing this had the benefit of seeing affinities of solidarity and exclusion. As Audre Lorde powerfully put it, "Any attack against Black people is a lesbian and gay issue, because I and thousands of other Black women are part of the lesbian community. Any attack against lesbians and gays is a Black issue, because thousands of lesbians and gay men are Black. There is no hierarchy of oppression."[55] Antiracism also extended into the legal profession, when a group of radical lawyer-scholars associated with the critical race theory (CRT) movement in the late 1970s sought to educate a generation of lawyers about the persistence of racism throughout the US legal and criminal justice system. CRT scholars helped students understand that the post-civil-rights dismantling of racial equality in the courts continued a long history in which material economic interests and political elite calculations were placed above concerns for racial equality. The legal profession's teaching of case law through abstract precedents and arguments was challenged. Narratives, stories, and experiences of black people were put in their place. Now students could begin to understand the formative historical role that law played in defining citizenship. CRT challenged the legal doctrine of "color blindness" by rendering its underlying presupposition false. Embedded naturalized white supremacy through the political system and in the deeply held, even if unconscious, assumptions of some juries, judges, and courts ensured that race would continue to play a role in administering justice.[56]

The First Black President

With antiracism circulating outside the public sphere from the 1970s through 2000s, no one could truly anticipate the result of the 2008 presidential election, which concluded with the election of the first black president, Barack Obama. Without question, white American dreams of postracialism and affirmations of goodwill rather than a serious commitment to antiracism may have led many whites to vote for someone whom black citizens supported in record numbers. Still, Obama's election was an important culmination of antiracist movements in the academy, where he developed intellectually. He devoured the political thought of King and Malcolm, had a self-described militant phase, and expressed admiration for the novels of Ralph Ellison and Toni Morrison. Obama's education as a law student at Harvard in the 1990s was influenced by CRT scholarship and black feminism. He embodied the nonviolent strategies of Bayard Rustin and the direct democratic activism of SNCC and Ella Baker through his community organizing in the working-class South Side of Chicago. This experience was clearly channeled in his 2008 presidential campaign—when young people across the country volunteered to canvass, speak to neighbors, and forge a network of local offices that brought him to elected office.[57]

But an important antiracist opportunity was nonetheless lost throughout his presidency. The participatory democratic energy that got him into office was never sustained or fully institutionalized beyond Election Day. Obama's charismatic appeal, like King's before him, created for some people the justification for political quietism. Their work was done. On-going direct struggle seemed unnecessary. Without question, Obama's ideology of centrist pragmatism—like Douglass's, the NAACP's, and the early King's before him—did not help push an agenda for transformative racial equality. In a sense, Obama missed an opportunity to seize the progressive space opened by a discredited political vision after Republican de-regulation efforts created the Great Recession in 2008 and eight years of a widely rebuked Bush presidency that led to two unpopular wars, in Afghanistan and Iraq, abroad and an expanding national security state at home. Obama's radical vision of "hope," which conjured an expansion of the New Deal and the Great Society programs, was replaced by a re-alistic agenda.

To be sure, even if this was more a strategic choice than an ideological commitment, Obama's centrism was, on some level, understandable—partly because as the first black president, the burden of respectability was especially pronounced. After all, Obama could not be "too black" or too critical and prophetic, even if he truly wanted to be. This is not even to mention that, throughout his presidency, he was racialized as un-American, foreign, too extreme, angry, and radical, in ways that recalled identical narratives about antiracists such as Douglass, Du Bois, Wells, King, and Malcolm. In the words of the right-wing commentator Dinesh D'Souza, in his best-selling *The Roots of Obama's Rage*, "The centrist Obama is gone and has been replaced by a more detached, unreadable, and, to some, even menac-ing Obama. . . . Obama and his team were moving America further away from the Lockean liberalism of the founders toward a more menacing Leviathan."[58]

But this characterization combined with an even more crucial development. From the moment Obama was elected until he left office in 2017, right-wing backlash was fervent. Led by the groundswell of opposition from a hard-core base of voters, Republican politicians obstructed Obama's policy agenda, refused to appoint his nominees to the federal courts, and constantly demonized what they falsely depicted as his totalitarian socialism and antiwhite worldview. Certainly, the passage of the Affordable Care Act (ACA) to guarantee health coverage for all Americans was incredibly valuable in moving beyond political rights to something much broader—like the Freedmen's Bureau, affirmative action, New Deal legislation, and the Fair Housing Act. Nonetheless—like those antiracist political acts—the ACA was deeply vulnerable to erosion without collective political will or concerted public action. Central to the ACA's construction was the libertarian philosophy of market-driven answers of a voucher system, rather than a single-payer universal care system, which did little to stem rising health costs. And like New Deal programs before it, the implementation of ACA was thus up to the whims of states, led by Republican majorities and leaders, who rejected Medicaid expansion on purely ideological and political grounds, even if—statistically—their relatively large percentage of uninsured citizens needed it the most. Working people—of whom there were many who are nonwhite—bore the brunt of this.

Obama had a mixed record on forging a progressive antiracist politics. He called for better labor protections and sought to eliminate gender-based pay disparity. But he never renounced faith in the free market or made a living wage of fifteen dollars per hour crucial to his agenda. He issued an executive order to protect undocumented children of immigrants, the so-called Dreamers, but engaged in deportations of undocumented people at unprecedented rates. He tried to end racial disparities in sentencing, and his Justice Department took up civil rights complaints and created consent decrees with police departments. But never did the Obama administration defend a bold vision to address the root causes of the school-to-prison pipeline: lack of funding for schools, militarized schools, and lack of community resources.

The Movement for Black Lives

Obama's presence in the public—like Douglass's, the NAACP's, and King's before him—created space for antiracist movements to form. The Black Lives Matter (BLM) movement was only nascent at the end of Obama's first term in 2012, after the killing in Florida of the young black teen Trayvon Martin by a neighborhood watchman, and only reached national prominence in the middle of his second term in 2014, after the killing of Michael Brown in Ferguson, Missouri. But BLM became a political force by the end of Obama's administration in 2016. Crucially, Obama never renounced the movement: he granted it legitimacy through his willingness to say publicly that if he had a son, he could easily look like Trayvon and by inviting BLM activists to a forum on policing at the White House.

But there was only so much legitimacy Obama could grant. The white backlash arguments against BLM followed a long history of reaction. In ways that were identical to what the civil rights movement faced, detractors claimed that BLM was antiwhite, that it prioritized the protection of black lives over white lives, that it demonized police officers, that it was uncivil and shrill in its arguments and unclear in its political demands. But BLM continued and synthesized historical antiracist tactics. What at first was a social media hashtag on Twitter, #BlackLivesMatter—developed by three queer women activists of color, Patrisse Cullors, Alicia Garza, and Opal Tometi—has since become a confederation of activists and organizations under the umbrella the Movement for Black Lives (MBL). At first, BLM activists protested in streets to reconfigure the meaning of democratic commitment in the hearts and minds of onlookers. Just as early slave revolts and civil rights actions defined protest as consistent with the aspiration of liberty, exemplary civic love was the justification given by BLM activists standing together before SWAT teams and a militarized police force in Ferguson after Michael Brown's killing and in Baltimore as a response to the twenty-five-year-old black man Freddie Gray's spine being dislocated while going for a "rough ride" under police custody in 2015.

Over the past several years, MBL organization has become more crucial to its strategy. It has embodied what Rustin once called the shift "from protest to politics."[59] Its initial placards and social media postings have now developed into an organization with a set of political demands defended by a coterie of young activists running for elected office. This antiracist work is especially important given that there has been a youth deficit in antiracist leadership, which has been generally wedded to a vision of democratic centrism that speaks the language of corporate America and legal equality rather than socioeconomic freedom. MBL has also followed SNCC's example of retaining the direct democratic energy of both young men and women and has internalized black feminism's intersectional thinking. MBL has done this while seizing the black radical call for economic equality and the Panthers' assault on police brutality. For this reason, appeals to shared interests with workers, women, Latinos, and Muslims have been invoked in the movement more than patriotic claims about liberal US national identity.

All this should hearten antiracists, but it is too soon to tell what political achievements MBL will realize, especially as it confronts a Trump presidency that is intent on using time-honored tactics of state-led repression—a recently exposed internal FBI report has warned of what the administration perceives as the threat of "Black Identity Extremism." As the leaked report states, "The FBI assesses it is very likely Black Identity Extremist (BIE) perceptions of police brutality against African Americans spurred an increase in premeditated, retaliatory lethal violence against law enforcement and will very likely serve as justification for such violence."[60] Nonetheless, antiracist history reveals that transformation takes time, even when it occurs. The antilynching movement never had any concrete political gains; radical labor activists had some, but they were uneven; and the civil rights movement took nine years from its inception to achieve a major legislative victory. But how should antiracist movements, such as MBL, confront this moment now, when the hope that glimmered so brightly with Obama's election seems all but lost?

Antiracist political history provides hope in dark times. Action is difficult, but it works—however slowly and unevenly. A less racist future has always seemed like a dream. But movements acted with the conviction and foresight that it was not a dream—with an imagination about what the future might be, even if it had not arrived yet. Violence, repression, and backlash were always present, but so was opportunity. Solidarities eroded, goals changed, leaders died, and movements disintegrated. But violence sometimes receded, and antiracist laws were eventually passed too. Repression became distracted, and new strategies were forged. Growing solidarity sometimes defeated backlash, and new coalitions were born. Moral and patriotic appeals sometimes moved white majorities to become antiracists, while shared-interest arguments broke down racial barriers. Reversals and failure were both guaranteed. The march was sometimes excruciating and frightening. But antiracists moved forward, always, despite the treacherous terrain and with an eye toward the future.

5

Antiracism Now

Antiracist thought and action is especially important now. White nationalists have been emboldened by Trump's presidency. Racial inequality remains disproportionate. Vulnerability is widespread, and democracy is under attack. Our moment needs citizens who defend racial justice, denounce white supremacy, and agitate for policies that achieve structural transformation. But what would this look like? What kinds of argument and politics would it entail?

Every antiracist must make his or her own political choices.[1] No singular vision can be generalized across the tradition, but shared themes exist. Antiracist thought is less of an ideology and more of a sensibility. It is defined by historical consciousness and attentiveness to social structure and political choices informed by power. Antiracist political thought is defined by a commitment to freedom, equality, and dignity. And antiracist political movements provide a blueprint for future action. The antiracist political tradition can help diminish contemporary racial inequality and energize freedom struggles across the world.

The Construction of Race

Antiracist thought refocuses attention on struggling against power extensively, rather than assuming that it is localized in the most obvious bad actors (the neo-Nazi or the white supremacist associated with the alt-right) or settings (blatant racist discrimination at work or on the streets). The antiracist knows that white supremacy is the foe toward which activists chant "Black Lives Matter," rather than individual white people. The chant is not meant to suggest that black people's lives matter more than others. Instead, it is meant to dramatize the unequal levels at which black people are subject to lethal state violence with little legal accountability[2] and the way they are disproportionately punished by a mass incarceration system, which has grown dramatically over the past three decades, even though crime has not.[3]

For this reason, the antiracist understands that when white people use words such as "nigger" to denigrate black people, it is not simply a "racial epithet" or "racially charged." The term is racist because it reinforces white supremacy, which has been targeted specifically at black people—not all people. This also explains why there is no moral equivalence between racism and antiracism. The confrontation between white-supremacist marchers in Charlottesville and antiracist protestors did not express "racial strife" or "racial tension" but a clear difference of intention. One group (white supremacists) wants to, and historically has tried time and time again to, exterminate and oppress the other (black people and racial minorities).

Antiracist thinking about social construction dismantles contemporary racist arguments. For instance, antiracists know that a willful distortion is behind the infamous claim of Richard Herrnstein and Charles Murray's *The Bell Curve* (1994) that black people's intelligence is naturally less than that of whites.[4] This is because social meaning, not innate biological difference, explains the racial education gap. Rubrics of success through standardized testing do not measure universal standards but what kinds of intelligence count as socially valuable (such as the skills of competition and individualism). Dominant white voices rather than marginalized nonwhite ones craft the education system.[5]

Beyond educational attainment, the construction of social meaning also explains why there is greater punishment of illegal acts in predominantly working-class black communities than of virtually identical acts in wealthier whites ones. A much harsher penalty is applied to the possession of cheap crystallized crack cocaine than to its more expensive counterpart in powdered form, used in affluent communities.[6] These are complex choices born out of racist histories. They do not describe reality but create it.

Historical Context

Antiracist historical awareness challenges claims that our moment is unprecedented. The constitutional system of checks and balances and the separation of powers has been used not only to protect against tyranny but to enact it. The Electoral College, which was partly designed to give southern slaveholding states disproportionate power in presidential elections, was precisely what allowed Trump to lose the popular vote by three million votes to Hilary Clinton but still become president. Furthermore, the Senate's design (two senators per state, regardless of population) gives less power to more populated, diverse, and multiracial states such as California and New York compared to predominantly rural and overwhelmingly homogeneously white and conservative states such as Wyoming, Idaho, and Montana.

Beyond the role of political institutions in perpetuating racial inequality, political elites who are now praised as the counterweight to Trump's racism in fact provided him a blueprint. Trump won on an explicitly white-nationalist campaign of "Make America Great Again" in 2016—a man whose political career began with the "birther myth" that Obama was a secret radical Muslim. But successful presidential campaigns in the post-civil-rights era not only have played on white people's perceived sense of victimhood but have been organized around the promise to contain crime—a notion that conjured, explicitly or implicitly, demonic images of black people. In 1988, George H. W. Bush's campaign circulated an image of a convicted black felon, Willie Horton, who was released on furlough and killed a white woman in Massachusetts. The purpose was to paint Bush's opponent— then the governor of the state, Michael Dukakis—as weak on crime. Four years later, Democrat Bill Clinton expressed his no-nonsense, centrist approach to crime during his presidential campaign in 1992 when, as governor, he flew to Arkansas to witness the execution of a mentally impaired black man,

Ricky Ray Rector. Two years later, Clinton doubled down, signing the Violent Crime Control and Law Enforcement Act of 1994, which exponentially increased law enforcement funding to continue the "War on Drugs" and hyperincarceration for black people that were begun by Ronald Reagan during his presidency in the 1980s.

Black disposability has also been mobilized for political gains. Consider, for instance, the attempt of then-senator Joe Biden, Democrat of Delaware, to cement his political centrism through his denunciation of the black law professor Anita Hill's public testimony and accusation of the sexual harassment she experienced at the hands of Clarence Thomas, in the latter's confirmation hearings to be appointed to the Supreme Court in 1991. Or more recently, consider the way Republican George W. Bush's apathetic response to the humanitarian disaster in New Orleans, after Hurricane Katrina, in 2005, reinforced his image as a no-nonsense conservative who took seriously states' rights, embraced personal responsibility, and refused to indiscriminately offer federal funds for disaster relief.[7]

Another prominent example of the presumptive devaluation of black knowledge is the Flint Water Crisis of 2016, which saw many children in the predominantly black city of Flint, Michigan, poisoned by lead-tainted drinking water.[8] The state of Michigan imposed an emergency manager to make unilateral decisions about public resources without consulting its citizens. Cost-cutting measures shifted the drinking-water source from the Detroit River to the Flint River, which corroded pipes that leeched lead into the water.

Fiscal austerity was placed above public health concerns and safety outcomes. But this was less significant than the state of Michigan's incredibly slow response, which took form only a year after initial reports surfaced and citizens' grievances were heard. One cannot help but infer that assumptions about black ignorance or playing the "victim card" led many officials to marginalize the concerns of black citizens who spoke up early and often, while their children's health was being permanently damaged.[9]

But racism has also paid rich dividends for conservative economic policy. The image of the "welfare queen" both helped Reagan push through massive cuts in federal social welfare programs in the 1980s and provided ammunition to political leaders who supported Clinton's deal with a right-wing Republican Congress to proudly dismantle "welfare as we know it" in 1996.[10] It should be remembered that business leaders who now despise Trump's lack of civility and "presidential etiquette" have remained silent during—if not tacitly or actively supported—attacks against government programs through playing on racialized notions of dependence. This is the idea— that is contradicted by the empirical evidence—that black people are the only ones who are "really" taking advantage of Medicaid, food assistance, and public housing programs.[11]

Beyond the way racism benefits political elites, antiracist thought reminds us that it has always been used to stabilize everyday white vulnerability. White people voted in droves for Trump, who refused to denounce the presidential endorsement of David Duke, a former Grand Wizard of the

Louisiana KKK. And some have even disseminated symbols of violence to black people today—nooses hung in locker rooms, racist graffiti in schools, death threats, and hate mail. The wage of whiteness (the idea that white skin offers a psychological wage of well-being and social status for white people, regardless of their socioeconomic resources) is especially high now.[12] After all, over the past three decades, white people's standard of living has exponentially decreased, good paying jobs are harder to find, and opioids are devastating rural and working-class white communities. Many lost their jobs, homes, and savings after the Great Recession of 2008 and the collapse of the housing market, created through deregulation and financial exploitation. Antiracism, however, supplies a rejoinder: Do not buy into the short-term gains of white supremacy. Instead, buy into the much longer-lasting and nourishing claim of collective power.[13]

Antiracist Structural Thinking

Understanding racism's structural historical legacies dismantles contemporary postracialism.[14] Two of the most prominent postracial arguments are usually posed as the following rhetorical questions: Slavery and Jim Crow are long gone, but why are black people still complaining? And, other immigrants (white ethnics from eastern Europe) came to the country with less resources than some black people have but have attained more wealth, so why do many black people refuse to take personal responsibility for their condition?

To these assertions, the antiracist would make two main claims. The first is that better laws aimed at nondiscrimination in the workplace are only part of the solution to years of accumulated socioeconomic disparity. What is necessary too (but missing from the public conversation) is redistributive programs that bring black citizens to an equal level to white citizens with respect to wealth, income, employment opportunity, housing, health outcomes, and educational achievement. The second is that white immigrants have had white skin and could assimilate as white. White skin granted them the ability to move to different neighborhoods, drop their ethnic-sounding surnames, and apply for good-paying jobs, without the stigmas associated with black skin. Black people, however, have always had black skin, on which they never could cash in on the open market to enrich themselves.[15]

Structural thinking about white supremacy also undermines racist interpretations of black life. Diminished opportunity and a lack of good-paying jobs, rather than "black laziness," explain black poverty.[16] Widespread gun access, promoted through the US gun lobby, the National Rifle Association (NRA), rather than the black cultural support of violence, explains the devastatingly high homicide rates in some black neighborhoods, in which gang membership is usually about a sense of belonging in lieu of well-funded cultural centers and thriving community spaces.[17] Inadequate state funding for deeply segregated predominantly black public schools, rather than black disinterest in learning, explains the educational achievement gap.[18] Homophobia and antiblack racism, not black sexual deviance, helps explain the disproportionate rate at which queer black people are subject to violence and trans women of color, in particular, are murdered.[19] Racism compounded with misogyny, lack of protection under the law, and unjust working environments—and not black women's inherent strength—explain why black women are affected by and continue to experience sexual violence (which is often dismissed) at higher rates than other women.[20]

From an antiracist perspective, it is thus equally necessary to see black rebellion (whether in Los Angeles, Detroit, or Newark in the 1960s or in some cities today) as a response to structural constraints such as poverty, police brutality, and mass incarceration rather than a reflection of cultural pathology.[21] Without question, it is possible to scrutinize, either on moral terms or on the basis of political efficacy, the violent activities of some antiracists—for instance, rioters in Ferguson after the Michael Brown killing in 2014 or in Baltimore after Freddie Gray's spine was dislocated in police custody in 2015. But for antiracists, this cannot be the exclusive response. This is because black rebellion is a manifestation of what Cornel West has called the problem of "nihilism in black America," the hopelessness facilitated by living amid massive inequality and deprivation within an apathetic white society.[22] The solution is not to put more people in jail but to create enlivening, life-affirming socioeconomic structures through which that nihilism could be countered.[23]

The Lived Experience of Racism

Antiracist awareness of racism's existentially diminishing and morally devaluing effects refocuses discussions about racial equality away from racial reconciliation to immediate political change. Highly publicized attempts at talking about race are certainly valuable symbolically for dramatizing that racism still matters. For instance, consider Obama's "beer summit" in 2009, in which he presided over a discussion between a distinguished African American Harvard University professor, Henry Louis Gates Jr., and a white police officer, who arrested Gates for trying to "break into" his own home. Or consider ongoing discussions about the meaning of race on campus, conversations that push students to uncover hidden assumptions and unacknowledged privileges. But from an antiracist perspective, these conversations can have unintended consequences when they become about "racial healing." This is because they moralize political problems and individualize collective problems, obscuring a more fundamental point: racism is not something to simply be eliminated in white or black people's minds but is an existential threat that determines not only blacks' self-perception and political freedom but their survival.

Antiracism allows us to see the dangerous distortions of racism. Black schoolchildren in the US are often not assumed to be just children having bad days but become threats that need to be disproportionately suspended, expelled, or thrown to the ground in classrooms across the country. Many black men are seen as clear and present dangers. Trayvon Martin, for example, is viewed as a dangerous intruder in a neighbor-hood in which he cannot possibly live, rather than a young black teen terrified, confused, and unsettled as he nervously holds a bag of Skittles while being followed by a neighbor-hood watchman simply for wearing a "suspicious" hoodie in Sanford, Florida, in 2012. The police officer Darren Wilson thinks he sees a hyperviolent "demon" when he shoots and kills an unarmed black teen, Michael Brown, in 2014.[24] Phi-lando Castile is not presumed to be a worker at a Montessori school in Minnesota in possession of a legal firearm but a trigger-happy, dreadlocked black man, ready to shoot anyone in his presence, so a Minneapolis officer shoots him in his car in 2016. Eric Garner is not seen as a black father selling loose cigarettes to earn money on a street in which he is both well known and well respected. Instead, he is seen as too unruly, before he is strangled for "resisting arrest" in 2014.

Similarly, Sandra Bland, a twenty-eight-year-old black woman, is perceived to be too unrepentant after a traffic violation in Texas in 2015 after she is arrested. After being found hanged in jail three days later, she is depicted as too emotionally weak, rather than debilitated by her experi-ence of racism. Glenda Gilmore, a black mother whose two children drown during Hurricane Sandy in 2012 because a white man refuses her shelter, seems much too imposing to be let in. Renisha McBride is not imagined to be a young woman in search of help but to be an immediate danger, before she is shot at point-blank range when she arrives at night at a white neighbor's doorstep in 2013 just outside De-troit, Michigan.[25]

Political Action

What, then, is to be done? Antiracist political theory supplies political solutions to contemporary racial inequality. The antiracist idea of freedom as self-determination means that black people should be able to walk the streets without the threat of violence. Achieving this would require serious substantive changes. Gone would be the lack of legal accountability for police officers who kill unarmed black men at radically unequal rates; "stop and frisk" laws that place black public space under constant police surveillance; "stand your ground" laws that allow citizens to shoot first and ask questions later; and death-row executions that disproportionately affect black people. Body cameras could provide a check on police power, and community oversight boards could provide a check on democratically unaccountable police departments.

But this would only be the beginning. Few political rights have been as essential for antiracists as the right to vote, over which there has been a long and contentious struggle. And over the past two decades, voting rights are again under attack through massive voter-disenfranchisement efforts led by Republican legislatures. Their efforts have been bolstered by the Supreme Court's monumental *Shelby County v. Holder* (2013), in which a conservative majority struck down one of the 1965 Voting Rights Act's most significant requirements— that states with histories of discrimination get federal preclearance to ensure compliance with federal voting law. From the antiracist perspective, a commitment to nondomination and equal rights means fighting against draconian voter-identification laws, which serve no purpose other than to disenfranchise. Alongside this struggle, it is necessary to argue for more accessible voting methods—such as online and absentee voting, same-day registration, and extended early voting, if not calling for a national voting holiday. Connected to this issue is defending fair, independent districting initiatives that combat gerrymandering, which over the past decade has enabled state legislators to carve out noncontiguous districts to erode popular voice. Despite losing the popular vote in the 2016 presidential election, Republicans in many states control all branches of state government.

Antiracists have long connected political rights to civil liberties. Antiracist pluralism means embracing political protest and free speech. Recent examples of this include Movement for Black Lives activists marching in the streets and athletes across the globe, inspired by the former NFL quarterback Colin Kaepernick, kneeling to protest the national anthem before games in 2016.

From the antiracist perspective, protests against white supremacists coming to campus are about standing for dignity and registering opposition to hierarchical, exclusionary, and violent ideologies—not simply opposing other people's free speech. Relatedly, student protests in the academy against Eurocentric curriculums are not assaults on faculty academic expertise but attempts to scrutinize the very purpose of education—not to police what counts as knowledge but to open it up to an ongoing democratic debate in which student voices can be considered. Moreover, dismantling Confederate monuments in public spaces does not erase racism from public consciousness but dismantles what those monuments represent: inequalities in public experience. This is about remaking a democratic public that is not defined by symbols of violence, genocide, and domination so that as many people feel welcome to freely walk the streets as possible. Antiracists know that what for white people is just bad public art or distasteful public memory is for people of color often a reminder of excruciating pain. It is less about special snowflakes griping about hurt feelings and more about politicizing what matters and who counts. Saying no to public racism remakes black voices as political agents rather than casualties of, or nonactors in, civic life.[26]

Yet political rights have rarely been sufficient in much antiracist thought. Social equality has been equally crucial. And over the past three decades, social equality has been under assault. There has been an evisceration of 1960s programs such as affirmative action in college admissions, integrated public schooling, and affordable-housing programs. To be sure, antiracists have debated the efficacy of all these programs. Does affirmative action do anything but benefit the "talented tenth," the cream of the crop, of black youth, while doing little, if anything, for many others languishing behind bars? Desegregation gives black children the opportunity to go to predominantly white schools but does nothing to encourage white children to go to predominantly black schools. Does this not simply reinforce unconscious white racism? How can fair housing counteract the ongoing legacy of centuries of economic domination?[27]

Objections such as these deserve more attention than is appreciated. But from an antiracist perspective, these incremental steps not only would alleviate massive inequality but could challenge the prevailing political orthodoxy of our time, which centers on more—rather than less—free markets, less social benefits, and more tax cuts for the superrich.[28] These antiracist policy initiatives can become the springboard from which to make, and to coexist alongside, more radical claims—about universal health care and Medicare for all, free college education, a living minimum wage, and the support of black cultural institutions. Freedom is not a one-size-fits-all project. It is also crucial to support policies that challenge intersectional oppression. Socioeconomic and cultural resources and legal protections are also necessary to deal with gender inequality, sexism, and homophobia throughout society.

Globalizing Antiracism

Antiracist thought is valuable for freedom struggles across the US beyond the issue of antiblack racism. The antiracist would see that Islamophobia creates a false link between racial identity and individual action. Muslim individuality and freedom are denied in favor of false psychological and cultural explanations that most Muslims support a culture of violence, which leads to terrorism on US soil. A prevailing American belief is that the religious idea of *jihad* in the Quran justifies acts of atrocity against non-Muslims or that Muslims have premodern, deeply misogynistic attitudes toward women.[29] Antiracists can dismantle these arguments by turning the tables on those who make these claims. Instead, they can point to the long history of US violence that needs to be systematically acknowledged and eliminated. Americans would need to come to terms with the domestic terrorism of antiblack racists such as Klansmen, neo-Nazis, and white nationalists who have partaken in the systemic brutalization of black citizens but also the genocidal polices toward Native Americans and the involvement in imperial wars abroad and a national security state at home. For antiracists, what would thus need to be dismantled is the widespread access to guns, the militarization of police forces and schools, and the expansion of prisons. Acknowledging the cultural prevalence of violence forces those who argue about "radical Islamic terrorism" into a difficult predicament—either they admit that American culture is crucially implicated in such violence, or they have to explain why Muslim people in particular are a unique case, a justification that turns on racist assumptions of inherent Muslim inferiority.[30]

Gender equality can also be defended on the antiracist grounds that it advances autonomy of both body and mind in ways not policed by patriarchy. This would mean fighting for women's reproductive rights and for better health care related to family planning. From the antiracist perspective, patriarchy would be emphasized as a structural matter to be addressed through better laws that create socioeconomic equality rather than merely cultural sensitivity. Eliminating the gender pay gap and federally funding maternity leave and child care would foster more freedom than sexual-harassment training in the workplace does.[31]

Hearing women's testimonies of rape and sexual assault would follow from the antiracist refusal to preemptively disauthorize narratives of dehumanization. All claims must be given space to be heard—especially those asserted by people whose experiences have long been silenced.[32] But at the same time, antiracists would likely be suspicious of structural power disparities being retold as problems of moral deviance. Too often, contemporary moralizing of powerful white men accused of sexual violence (they are called "predators") recalls the demonizing language that lynchers used against black men and that of "superpredators" that Bill Clinton invoked to justify the passage of the 1994 Violent Crime Control Act.[33] No doubt, sexual violence requires vigorous and concerted exposure and political opposition. But the language of moral deviance polices the boundaries of community—who is seen as normal and who is not. Such binary thinking promotes a hierarchical worldview. From the antiracist perspective, challenging this is crucial not only because of the present but for the future. Now, it is powerful white men who are its subjects. But inevitably it will be the socially demonized groups toward whom it has always been directed: black people, brown people, and queer people. Moreover, what for white male "predators" is public embarrassment and loss of employment for these people will likely be police brutality, mass incarceration, homophobic hate crime, and mass deportations.[34]

In addition to gender equality, antiracists could defend undocumented people's rights through the idea that political inclusion must be based on prioritizing human dignity, not national security. Socioeconomic forces that create a mass market for drugs in the US belie calls for tougher border security. Responsibility lies with low wages, a destroyed industrial sector, and the evisceration of the welfare state—not some imagined Mexican culture of crime.[35] Antiracists can further leverage economic arguments about citizenship. Arguing that undocumented people's labor—like slave labor in the antebellum period and sharecropping during Jim Crow—has been crucial to building the US economy can help make a claim on equal citizenship.[36] Anti-Latino racism can also be undermined through the antiracist idea of cultural hybridity. Talk of English-language purity or English-only teaching in public schools is a nostalgic fantasy that does not correspond to reality when Spanish-speaking citizens constitute the vast majority of students in many schools. A commitment to democracy means that these citizens should have their language and culture recognized because they are the citizens whose authority elected officials must respect.[37]

Much can be said about globalizing antiracism beyond US borders. Syrian refugees would be seen as fellow citizens worthy of human rights rather than aliens deserving of pity. Struggle would be waged on behalf of queer men and women across the world experiencing daily insecurity and violence. Solidarity would be expressed with Palestinians experiencing an unjust Israeli occupation in the West Bank and Gaza and the millions of enslaved people—the laborers, sex workers, migrants—and prisoners (political or otherwise) across the world who have no freedom to speak of.[38]

In the final analysis, the success of such a contemporary antiracist politics would be more likely if many nonracist white Americans broaden their understanding of political theory to include black antiracism. Without question, black antiracism is a unique response to the black American experience. But its political ideas dramatize what is entailed in the shift from innocence to awareness, from nonracism to antiracism. Taking black antiracism seriously would mean white people examining why they never worry that a police encounter could easily turn deadly, why paying lip service to equal rights is not the same as committing oneself to desegregation through school integration or the inclusion of black voices and students on campus, or why there is something racist about personally believing that black people must constantly prove or justify their intelligence or equal moral worth to be taken seriously. This kind of intellectual awakening is important. But it is not enough. It is equally necessary for white people to support transformative public policies and become involved in interracial struggles and coalitions to make them real.

Antiracism Today

Antiracist political movements face an uphill battle today. The Trump administration has, in a relatively short time, rolled back or invalidated much of Obama's racial justice efforts. Consent decrees with police departments (legal agreements between the Department of Justice and local authorities about certain practices and policies) relating to racial discrimination and excessive police force have been annulled, and police officers have been encouraged to be "rough" in their encounters with communities.[39] There is a renewed push to privatize prisons at higher rates,[40] and school vouchers have been championed over public school funding.[41] And there are also the administration's rescinding of DACA, the US travel ban on citizens from seven majority-Muslim nations, and the increased deportations of undocumented people by federal immigration agents. Unlike Obama, Trump's goal is to close as much space as possible for antiracist movements to form. Our conservative moment, defined by the Trump presidency, has produced a sense of heightened precariousness for the most vulnerable citizens: black people, Muslims, undocumented people, LGBTQ people, sick people, poor people, and incarcerated people.

But a silver lining nonetheless exists. And antiracists could exploit political opportunities today. Over the past several years, there has been a growing public consensus against right-wing views on economic policy, mass incarceration, immigration, and reproductive and gay rights. Tremendous possibility thus exists for the formation of new political majorities, in which antiracists play a crucial part. New social movements have been on the rise: the Women's March in Washington in 2017, the Fight for Fifteen movement, the Dakota Access Pipeline protests, the Sanctuary Campus movement, United We Dream, #MeToo, and, most recently, the student activists associated with #NeverAgain, which was organized by high school survivors of a mass school shooting in Parkland, Florida, in February 2018 that left seventeen people dead. Attacking racism could be made a central platform in these struggles, while antiracists could join them with the same energy they direct toward their own. They can link up with white allies working to disidentify with their white privilege and social power, undocumented workers struggling for human rights, queer people resisting homophobia, feminists arguing for gender equality and reproductive rights, and environmentalists fighting willful apathy toward global warming. As antiracist history has shown, there is strength in numbers, and the broader the banner and the more people involved, the more likely it is to succeed.

Antiracist communication tools have evolved since the 1960s. Television and radio have been replaced with social media and live streaming technology, which disseminates ideas in a more expansive and faster way than ever before.[42] But direct action is still essential. Marches, boycotts, protests, and sit-ins can help force elites to the negotiating table and make visible demands for socioeconomic equality and freedom. Antiracists and their allies could mobilize by forcing Democratic politicians who defend antiracism in theory but stop short of endorsing it in practice (such as abolishing the mass incarceration state, massive economic inequality, and lack of well-funded social welfare programs) to make the same choice activists forced in the 1960s. They can either make a serious effort to accept the demands of their constituents or risk losing their votes. Disruption has been hailed as the new method of economic innovation, but the truth is, its political manifestation is deeply threatening to elite power. This fear of collective action is vividly displayed through the recent attempt of several Republican state legislatures to criminalize public protest (though they ultimately failed, some have tried to pass bills that exonerate drivers who mow down nonviolent protestors blocking traffic).[43] This is precisely why such protest has often worked historically.

There is antiracist value in the corporate push against the Trump administration's ban on citizens of seven majority-Muslim countries visiting the US. But this distracts from the lengths many corporations go to prevent unionization—through misinformation campaigns and antiunion arguments—and from the states that have draconian restrictions on the legality of work stoppages.

Whatever form contemporary antiracism takes, the crucial thing is that the struggle be visible and public, loud and clear, with a sense of political vision and conviction. Above all else, what matters is that it is ongoing. No matter the scope, location, or level of intensity, the antiracist flame needs to burn brightly. Antiracism has always been tasked with confronting the present, but it has always contested the meaning of the future. Not only has antiracism always assumed a future that could be otherwise, but in doing so, it has given hope to future generations.[44] It has always been a message in a bottle to future citizens who might find its vision washed up on a distant shore. It is impossible say what the future might bring. But if antiracism embodies the legacy of its historical lineage, there always exists a sense of imaginative, transformative possibilities. And that has never been a small thing.

ACKNOWLEDGMENTS

This book would have been impossible without the encouragement and support of many people who dedicated time and energy throughout the process. I would like to thank my editor, Ilene Kalish, whose initial support for the project was crucial and whose keen editorial eye and thoughtful comments vastly improved the finished product. Thanks too to Maryam Arain and all of the people at NYU Press, who helped at every stage throughout the process. I am also especially grateful to the two anonymous reviewers for NYU who took the time to carefully engage the book and offered incisive feedback and comments that sharpened its focus, its scope, and the arguments it tries to make.

My colleagues and friends also deserve special thanks. Thanks to Elvira Basevich and Jeffrey Broxmeyer for reading drafts of the work, and thanks for all the many conversations with Michael Barry, Max Burkey, Erin Dwyer, Karl Ericson, Arthur Getman, Mary-Catherine Harrison, Michelle Jacobs, Jon Keller, Matt Kirkpatrick, Kevin Laam, Stephen Manning, Susan McCarty, Dave Merolla, Genevieve Meyers, Mark Navin, Nicholas Rombes, Rosemary Weatherston, and Rodger Wyn. Special thanks to Christopher Clark for the research assistance. Thanks, as always to, my extended family—Grace Hamilton, who generously read a draft of the manuscript, and to Frona Powell, Ron Powell, Aaron Powell, Liz Powell, Arnold Zamalin, Marina Zamalin, Emil Zamalin, and Raya Zamalin.

This book would not have been written without the unconditional support of Alison Powell, who continues to inspire me with her beautiful intellect and boundless love. And to my children, Sam and Anita: your presence in my life has pushed me to be a better person in ways you cannot imagine and to always maintain hope about what the future might bring.

NOTES

CHAPTER 1. THE ORIGINS OF AMERICAN ANTIRACISM

1. See Trump, "Full Text." For a contemporary account of the rise of white supremacy today, see Hawley, *Making Sense of the Alt-Right*.

2. See Fredrickson, *Racism*, 56–57.

3. For an intellectual history of racism, see Rattansi, *Racism*; for a theoretical account, see Memmi, *Racism*; for an existential account, see L. Gordon, *Bad Faith and Antiblack Racism*. For one that focuses on anti-Semitism, see Sartre, *Anti-Semite and Jew*; and for racism under colonialism, see Fanon, *Wretched of the Earth*. For an account that complicates the story told by Fredrickson and details how the racist ideas and thinking evident in modernity originated much earlier, see Isaac, *Invention of Racism in Classical Antiquity*. For the interaction between racism and slavery, see D. Davis, *Slavery and Human Progress*; for slavery in the United States, see Kolchin, *American Slavery*; for Jim Crow, see Litwack, *Trouble in Mind*.

4. For the history of racist ideas and structures of thinking in America, see Kendi, *Stamped from the Beginning*. For an excellent political theoretical account of how racism works in the contemporary US, see McKnight, *Everyday Practice of Race in America*; and McKnight, *Race and the Politics of Exception*. For an account that argues that socioeconomic inequality—and the practice of racism through political institutions—is what creates the illusion of racial difference, see Fields and Fields, *Racecraft*. For a philosophical argument about the salience of racial identity in making epistemological claims about society and politics, see Alcoff, *Visible Identities*.

5. For example, in Paul Gilroy's now classic *Against Race*, he invokes antiracism as an implicit opposite to what he powerfully criticizes, racial thinking's dominance—on the political left and right—since World War II. But the book does not fully articulate what it truly means to be antiracist politically or what antiracist political thought

entails. In arguing that antiracism contains a philosophical vision, this book contributes to the attempt to excavate the political theory of black political thought.

6. Over the past several years, and especially after Trump's election and the Women's March in Washington to protest his inauguration, there has been an upsurge in thinking about the politics of resistance. See Klein, *No Is Not Enough*. For a specific focus on black politics today, see Taylor, *From #BlackLivesMatter to Black Liberation*. For an account that unpacks the ideas that emerge from black resistance, see Zamalin, *Struggle on Their Minds*.

7. To be sure, racism against Native Americans in the US, in a certain sense, existed prior to antiblack racism and was a crucial justification for land expropriation and violence against native peoples before and alongside antiblack racism from the seventeenth century onward. For a study that examines racism against Native American people, see Smith, *Conquest*. For a political theoretical account, see Rogin, *Fathers and Children*.

8. For the way in which immigration policy has been racialized and the processes through which antiblack policies and ideas have fractured political solidarities, see Hattam, *In the Shadow of Race*. For an account of how whiteness became an ideal to which many white ethnics aspired, see Jacobsen, *Whiteness of a Different Color*; and Jacobsen, *Roots Too*.

9. This book differs from that of the historian Herbert Aptheker's important *Anti-Racism in US History* because it offers an overview of antiracist political thought in major black movements and thinkers, rather than restricting the analysis to white antislavery allies in the first two hundred years of American history. Furthermore, although Kendi's *Stamped from the Beginning* is an excellent primer on racist and antiracist ideas, his primary focus is on several major figures such as Cotton Maher, Thomas Jefferson, William Lloyd Garrison, W. E. B. Du Bois, and Angela Davis, and the book is a historical exploration of the evolution of such ideas over time. This text, however, offers an account of antiracism as a political theory and focuses its scope much more broadly and politically.

10. For a recent selection of work written by political theorists, see Gooding-Williams, *In the Shadow of Du Bois*; Balfour, *Democracy's Reconstruction*; Turner, *Awakening to Race*; Bromell, *Time Is Always Now*; Lebron, *Black Lives Matter*; Hooker, *Theorizing Race in the Americas*; and Threadcraft, *Intimate Justice*.

11. This book is intended to introduce readers to an important tradition, as Richard Delgado and Jean Stefancic's *Critical Race Theory* and Patricia Hill Collins and Sirma Bilge's *Intersectionality* are. Although written as a brief intellectual history, this book follows recent work on the kind of citizenship necessary to confront racial inequality. See Turner, *Awakening to Race*; Allen, *Talking to Strangers*; Bromell, *Time Is Always Now*; Zamalin, *Struggle on Their Minds*.

12. In this way, the book tries to isolate a certain intellectual worldview that can animate political thinking today, as does Paget Henry's seminal work, *Caliban's Reason*, as well as Stephen Eric Bronner's *Reclaiming the Enlightenment*.

13. For a more explicit account of how art and politics were fused in antiracist struggle, see Iton, *In Search of the Black Fantastic*; Moten, *In the Break*; Watts, *Amiri Baraka*; Kelley, *Yo' Mama's Disfunktional!*; Sharpe, *In the Wake*.

14. For a study of prophetic rhetoric for black liberation, see Marshall, *City on the Hill from Below*; West, *Prophesy Deliverance!*; Glaude, *Exodus!*

15. For what still remains the canonical study on the Western tradition, see Wolin, *Politics and Vision*.

16. This point is implicitly detailed through Lewis Gordon's *Introduction to Africana Philosophy* and through theoretical "creolization" of Afro and Euro perspectives in Jane Gordon's *Creolizing Political Theory*, as well as Gordon and Neil Roberts's *Creolizing Rousseau*.

17. For the liberal tradition in American culture, see Hartz, *Liberal Tradition in America*; and Hofstadter, *American Political Tradition*. For a classic defense of liberal political thought, see Locke, *Second Treatise of Government*; and Rawls, *Theory of Justice*. For a historical overview of liberal political theory, see Freeden, *Liberalism*. For an

argument about the link between liberalism and exclusion, see Mehta, *Liberalism and Empire*.

18. For an excellent argument about the way theories of freedom under those who experience constraint are different from those who do not, see Roberts, *Freedom as Marronage*. For a contemporary defense of these visions from a black, radical, liberal perspective, see Mills, *Black Rights / White Wrongs*.

19. For a study of the core ideologies of black political thought—black disillusioned liberal, socialist, Marxist, conservative, radical egalitarian, and black feminist—see Dawson, *Black Visions*. For the way these ideologies play out in black public opinion and the idea of shared black fate, see Dawson, *Behind the Mule*.

20. By "conservatism," I am referring here to the tradition in the US that defends the values of tradition and established social convention. If, however, one argues that a certain strain of contemporary US conservatism is based on defending market rationality and privatization, then it is true that one can find some black Americans who have held a faith in the market and private property for solving the problem of racism (e.g., Garvey, Washington, early Malcolm X, and Ida B. Wells). For a study that accepts this definition as its premise, see Lilla, *Shipwrecked Mind*.

21. For this position from the perspective of conservative political thought, which emphasizes the way the tradition is less about order and stability and more about disruption and an energetic defense of hierarchy and inequality by any means necessary, see Robin, *Reactionary Mind*.

22. For an account of how racism was integral to the development of modern conservatism, see Lowndes, *From the New Deal to the New Right*. For the way it worked in the construction of the social welfare state, see Lieberman, *Shifting the Color Line*; and for a comparative perspective, see Lieberman, *Shaping Race Policy*.

23. Obama, "More Perfect Union."

24. See B. Washington, "Standard Printed Version of the Atlanta Exposition Address."

25. See Ferguson, *Sage of Sugar Hill*.

26. "Meredith Appears," 28.

27. Thrush, "Under Ben Carson."
28. Stack, "Ben Carson Refers to Slaves as 'Immigrants,'" A13.
29. For an account of radical democracy in America, see Frank, *Constituent Moments*. For a contemporary anthology of collected writings on radical democratic theory, see Trend, *Radical Democracy*. For a classic account of radical democracy, see Mouffe, *Democratic Paradox*.
30. For what still remains a classic text on the golden age of social democratic thought in America, see Kloppenberg, *Uncertain Victory*.
31. For an excellent critique and philosophical exploration of the failure and potential for white antiracism, see Alcoff, *Future of Whiteness*.
32. For contemporary accounts of this position, see McWhorter, *Winning the Race*; and Steele, *Shame*.
33. A version of this argument has been advanced by the black radical Adolph Reed, whose book *Class Notes: Posing as Politics and Other Notes on the Class Scene* (2001) is still applicable today. The most conspicuous critique of the opposition between focusing on class and focusing on race for liberation, however, is Cedric Robinson's *Black Marxism*.
34. It is no wonder that the Southern Poverty Law Center has reported that racist hate crimes jumped noticeably in 2016, when Trump's campaign was in full swing. For an account of this statistic, as well as the rise of extremist hate groups in 2016, see Southern Poverty Law Center, *Intelligence Report*, 162.
35. A dated, but nonetheless still relevant, encapsulation of this kind of argument is D'Souza, *End of Racism*.
36. The long history of cultural pathology arguments, dating back to the end of the nineteenth century, is found in Scott, *Contempt and Pity*. For an account of how this view was reproduced through the work of one of the twentieth century's most prominent social scientists, Gunnar Myrdal, see Jackson, *Gunnar Myrdal and America's Conscience*. For a contemporary survey and, even if not a completely successful, critique of some of these views, see Wilson, *More than Just Race*. For a more compelling critique from the perspective of moral philosophy, see Shelby, *Dark Ghettos*.

CHAPTER 2. REJECTING THE POWER OF RACISM

1. Lorde, "Scratching the Surface," 45.
2. Ture and Hamilton, *Black Power*, 3.
3. Quoted in Martin, *Mind of Frederick Douglass*, 88.
4. Wells, "Lynch Law in America," 401.
5. Baraka, *Somebody Blew Up America*, 49.
6. Walker, *Appeal*, 5.
7. King, "Love, Law, and Civil Disobedience," 47.
8. A. Davis, *Freedom Is a Constant Struggle*, 4.
9. For a classic contemporary account of the way race is sociologically constituted, see Omi and Winant, *Racial Formation in the United Sates*.
10. For an account of this idea, see Norton, *95 Theses on Politics, Culture, and Method*.
11. Delany, *Condition*, 19.
12. Walker, *Appeal*, 8.
13. Fortune, *Black and White*, 15.
14. Baldwin, "Nobody Knows My Name," 188.
15. Baldwin, "Words of a Native Son," 400.
16. Walker, *Appeal*, 18.
17. Baldwin, "We Can Change This Country," 60.
18. Du Bois, *Black Reconstruction*, 700. For a historical example of this idea, see Morgan, *American Slavery, American Freedom*; and Roediger, *Wages of Whiteness*.
19. Quoted in J. Perry, *Hubert Harrison*, 147.
20. Du Bois, *Gift of Black Folk*, x.
21. Douglass, "Constitution of the United States."
22. Wells, *Red Record*, 225.
23. Ibid.
24. King, "Letter from Birmingham City Jail," 295.
25. Delany, *Condition*, 31.
26. Malcolm X and Haley, *Autobiography of Malcolm X*, 38.
27. Bell, "Unintended Lessons in *Brown v. Board of Education*," 1059.
28. For an account of the what Charles Mills importantly defines as the epistemology of ignorance, see *Racial Contract*.
29. Baldwin, *The Fire Next Time*, 2.
30. Du Bois, *Souls of Black Folk*, 8.

31. Lorde, "Age, Race, Class, and Sex," 117; see also Lorde, "Master's Tools."
32. Ellison, "Extravagance of Laughter," 639.
33. Baldwin, "Many Thousands Gone," 66.
34. Malcolm X, letter to the editor.
35. Du Bois, *Darkwater*, 32.
36. A. Davis, "Prison-Industrial Complex," 38.
37. Ture and Hamilton, *Black Power*, 37.
38. Larsen, *Passing*, 30.
39. Baldwin, "Many Thousands Gone," 66.
40. Cone, *Black Theology of Liberation*, xviii.
41. Schuyler, *Black No More*, 88–89.
42. Jones, *Dutchman*, 31.
43. Ibid., 35.
44. Du Bois, *Souls of Black Folk*, 50.
45. Obama, "Barack Obama's Speech on Race."
46. See Katznelson, *When Affirmative Action Was White*; Lieberman, *Shifting the Color Line*; Massey and Denton, *American Apartheid*; Oliver and Shapiro, *Black Wealth, White Wealth*.
47. This is the point made by the contemporary sociologist Eduardo Bonilla-Silva in *Racism without Racists*.
48. Ture and Hamilton, *Black Power*, 155.
49. A. Davis, "Meaning of Freedom," 141.
50. A. Locke, "New Negro," 15.
51. Jones, *Blues People*, x–xi.
52. Ellison, "Little Man at Chehaw Station," 505.
53. West, "Black Strivings in a Twilight Civilization," 118.
54. H. Rap Brown, press conference at the Student Nonviolent Coordinating Committee headquarters, Washington, DC, July 27, 1967, as reported by the *Evening Star*, July 27, 1967, 1.
55. Hughes, "Let America Be America Again," 191.
56. Douglass, "Meaning of July Fourth," 196.
57. See J. Locke, *Second Treatise*; and Rawls, *Theory of Justice*.
58. Du Bois, *Souls of Black Folk*, 8.
59. Douglass, "Meaning of July Fourth," 196.
60. Calhoun, "Speech on the Reception of Abolition Petitions," 630.
61. Stewart, "Address Delivered at the African Masonic Hall," 63.

62. Ture and Hamilton had incommensurable disagreements with King about black political strategy, but they agreed with him on this: "Those responses are luxuries for people with time to spare. . . . Black people in America have no time to play nice" (*Black Power*, xvii).
63. King, "Letter from Birmingham City Jail," 293.
64. Coates, *Between the World and Me*, 9.
65. Cooper, *Voice from the South*, 62.
66. Collins, *Black Feminist Thought*, 221. Multiple layers of oppression that black women have experienced because of classism, gender discrimination, homophobia, ageism, and ableism made it impossible to recognize the intersectional needs of black women. Racist patriarchy at once devalued black women's political oppression while assigning them a saintly status in which their human vulnerability was denied. See also Lorde, *Sister/Outsider*; James and Sharpley-Whiting, *Black Feminist Reader*.
67. Crenshaw, "Mapping the Margins."
68. Quoted in Stetson and David, *Glorying in Tribulation*, 54.
69. Even black nationalists who disengaged with white elites and institutions politically agreed with this claim. See D. Robinson, *Black Nationalism*.
70. Malcolm X, "America's Gravest Crisis," 71.
71. King, "Letter from Birmingham City Jail," 295.
72. This idea prompted Baldwin to say that white people "bear an inescapable responsibility" for the present, "but since in the main they seem to lack the energy to change this condition they would rather not be reminded of it" ("White Man's Guilt," 409).
73. Bell, *Faces at the Bottom of the Well*, x.

CHAPTER 3. FIGHTING FOR FREEDOM
1. Douglass, "Meaning of July Fourth," 196.
2. Baldwin, "Stranger in the Village," 88.
3. Malcolm X, roundtable.
4. Malcolm X, "Speech at University of California, Berkeley."
5. Hamer, *Speeches of Fannie Lou Hamer*, 73.
6. Simone, "I Wish I Knew How It Feels to Be Free."
7. Douglass, *Autobiographies*, 598.

8. Morrison, *Beloved*, 162.
9. Sumner, *What Social Classes Owe to Each Other*.
10. For an elaboration of this important point, see Turner, *Awakening to Race*, 58.
11. Randolph, "Address at the March on Washington," 262–263.
12. Forman, "Black Manifesto."
13. See R. Robinson, *Debt*.
14. For a sample curriculum of Freedom Schools, see Emery, Braselmann, and Gold, "Introduction."
15. For an overview of Liberation Schools, see Bloom and Martin, *Black against Empire*, 192–193. See also Nelson, Thomas, and Garcha, "Liberation Schools."
16. Moses and Cobb, *Radical Equations*.
17. Carmichael, *Ready for Revolution*, 391.
18. A. Locke, "New Negro," 15.
19. Sun Ra, *Immeasurable Equation*, 128.
20. Baldwin, *The Fire Next Time*, 91.
21. Wright, "Blueprint for Negro Writing," 201.
22. Ellison, *Invisible Man*, 1.
23. Baldwin, "Many Thousands Gone," 77.
24. Quoted in Campbell, "Revolution Song."
25. Morrison, *Paradise*, 308.
26. Lorde, "Uses of the Erotic," 57.
27. Ellison, "*American Dilemma*," 339.
28. See Moses, *Golden Age of Black Nationalism*; Stuckey, *Ideological Origins of Black Nationalism*.
29. For a history of these leadership ideas, see Gaines, *Uplifting the Race*.
30. E. Baker, "Developing Community Leadership," 351.
31. The best history of SNCC is Payne, *I've Got the Light of Freedom*.
32. Malcolm X, "Bullet or the Ballot," 33.
33. King, "Case against 'Tokenism,'" 109.
34. King, "Rising Tide," 150.
35. King "Experiment in Love," 19.
36. Baldwin, "American Dream and the American Negro."
37. For Baldwin's argument for self-examination, see *The Fire Next Time*.

38. Quoted in J. Perry, *Hubert Harrison*, 194.
39. Prison Research Education Action Project, *Instead of Prisons*.
40. Movement for Black Lives, "Platform."
41. Lorde, "Master's Tools," 111.
42. Baraka, *"Pan-African Party and the Black Nation,"* 26.
43. Malcolm X, "Not Just an American Problem," 182.
44. King, "Letter from Birmingham City Jail," 147.
45. King, "Time to Break Silence," 233.
46. Newton, "Intercommunalism," 188.
47. Wells, "Ida B. Wells Case."
48. King, "Letter from Birmingham City Jail," 291.
49. Ibid., 294.
50. Jacobson, "Claudette Colvin Explains Her Role."
51. Jacobs, *Incidents in the Life of a Slave Girl*, 70.
52. For an excellent discussion of this idea, see Roberts, *Freedom as Marronage*.
53. A. Davis, *Freedom Is a Constant Struggle*.
54. Dunbar, "Sympathy," 102.
55. O. Davis, "Eulogy of Malcolm X," 310.
56. For the finest treatment of this subject, see Winters, *Hope Draped in Black*.
57. Randolph, "Address at the March on Washington," 110.
58. West, *Race Matters*, 109.
59. King, *"Playboy* Interview," 352.
60. King, "Letter from Birmingham City Jail," 295.
61. West, *Race Matters*, 8.

CHAPTER 4. POLITICAL MOVEMENTS IN STRUGGLE

1. Aptheker, *American Negro Slave Revolts*; Genovese, *From Rebellion to Revolution*.
2. For the best sociological argument about the power of disruptive protest, see Piven and Cloward, *Poor People's Movements*.
3. Garnet, "Address to the Slaves of the United States of America."
4. For a recent history, see Foner, *Gateway to Freedom*.
5. As Foner writes, "Estimates—guesses really—suggest somewhere between 1,000 and 5,000 per year between 1830 and 1860" (ibid., 4).

6. For an excellent collection of essays dealing with the historical emergence and roots of the public sphere, see Black Public Sphere Collective, *Black Public Sphere*.

7. Stewart, "Lecture Delivered at Franklin Hall," 48.

8. Douglass, "Meaning of July Fourth," 190.

9. For a conceptual critique of this point, see Burkey and Zamalin, "Patriotism, Black Politics and Racial Justice in America."

10. See Garnet, "Address to the Slaves of the United States of America."

11. For a history of Reconstruction and its betrayal, see Foner, *Reconstruction*.

12. See Turner, *Awakening to Race*, 57.

13. See Du Bois, *Black Reconstruction in America*.

14. See Keyssar, *Right to Vote*, 74–93.

15. B. Washington, "Standard Printed Version," 585.

16. For this story, see Litwack, *Trouble in Mind*.

17. On Du Bois's life and politics, see Lewis, *W. E. B. Du Bois*.

18. For a history of the NAACP, see Kellogg, *NAACP*.

19. See Waldrep, *African Americans Confront Lynching*.

20. Fortune, *Black and White*, 106.

21. In this way, Wells's arguments resonated with the burgeoning suffragist and women's rights movements of the time. For Wells's politics, see Bay, *To Tell the Truth Freely*; and for her political thought, see Zamalin, *Struggle on Their Minds*, chap. 2.

22. Wells, *Southern Horrors*, 62.

23. For an intellectual history of black Marxism, see C. Robinson, *Black Marxism*. For a philosophical exploration, see Mills, *From Class to Race*.

24. See Winders, "New Deal Agricultural Policy."

25. Quoted in Fredrickson, *Black Liberation*, 140.

26. Stevens, *Red International and Black Caribbean*.

27. See Kelley, *Hammer and Hoe*.

28. Rawley, *Richard Wright*, 291–292.

29. Marable, *Race, Rebellion, and Reform*.

30. See Hall, "Long Civil Rights Movement."

31. For an account of civil rights politics, see Luders, *Civil Rights Movement*.

32. For an excellent history of this period, see Dudziak, *Cold War Civil Rights*.

33. King, "I Have a Dream," 217.

34. Morris, *Origins of the Civil Rights Movement*. For an interpretation of this idea and an argument about the way the movement tried to reconstruct the meaning of the civil sphere, see J. Alexander, *Civil Sphere*, 265–394.

35. See Morris, *Origins of the Civil Rights Movement*.

36. For an interpretation of the radical King, see Mantler, *Power to the Poor*.

37. E. Baker, "Bigger than a Hamburger," 4.

38. For a general overview of SNCC, see Payne, *I've Got the Light of Freedom*; and Carson, *In Struggle*.

39. Ture, "Berkeley Speech," 49.

40. For a study of SNCC's radicalization, see McAdam, *Political Process*, 181–229.

41. See D. Robinson, *Black Nationalism*.

42. For more on Garvey and UNIA, see Stein, *Marcus Garvey*.

43. Malcolm X, *By Any Means Necessary*, 37.

44. The best account of Malcolm's life and politics is Marable, *Malcolm X*.

45. See Bloom and Martin, *Black against Empire*; and Jeffries, *Huey P. Newton*.

46. Brown, *Taste of Power*, 5.

47. Newton, "Women's Liberation and Gay Liberation Movements," 158.

48. National Advisory Commission on Civil Disorders, *Kerner Report*, 52.

49. For a history of this retreat, see Steinberg, *Turning Back*.

50. For this history, see H. Baker, *Betrayal*.

51. Afrocentric thought was controversial—like earlier forms of black cultural nationalism that promised black spiritual rebirth through connecting to a forgotten, pre-slave African past. But it nonetheless tried to unsettle expectations about black identity and thought. See Asante, *Afrocentricity*.

52. Combahee River Collective, "Black Feminist Statement," 214.

53. See Mary Helen Washington's *Invented Lives: Narratives of Black Women, 1860–1960*, which recovered the unique tradition of black

women's voices and lives; Patricia Hill Collins's *Black Feminist Thought*; and Angela Davis's *Women, Race, and Class*, which described the formative role of gender, race, and capitalism in reproducing racial patriarchy in the United States and fracturing the women's movement.

54. hooks, *Ain't I a Woman?*, 13.
55. Lorde, "There Is No Hierarchy of Oppression," 220.
56. See Bell, *Voices at the Bottom of the Well*; and Delgado and Stefancic, *Critical Race Theory*.
57. For an account of Obama, see Kloppenberg, *Reading Obama*; and King and Smith, *Still a House Divided*.
58. D'Souza, *Roots of Obama's Rage*, 2, 6.
59. Rustin, "From Protest to Politics."
60. Winter and Weinberger, "FBI's New Terrorist Threat."

CHAPTER 5. ANTIRACISM NOW

1. Transposing arguments from the past onto the present carries the risk of oversimplification. Further complicating the matter is that antiracist arguments were always animated in defense of specific political visions and policy goals. The antiracist communist wanted an abolition of capitalism, the socialist better worker control in the workplace, the liberal more political rights, the feminist less patriarchy, the cosmopolitan more human rights, and the antiwar activist peace. Nonetheless, historical ideas can enliven the present, as Sheldon Wolin has famously argued in *Politics and Vision*.
2. For a journalistic overview of this subject—which has become especially visible through high-profile killings of unarmed black men and women over the past decade—see Lowery, *They Can't Kill Us All*.
3. For this argument, see M. Alexander, *New Jim Crow*. For a history of the construction of mass incarceration and its disproportionate impact on black Americans, see Murakawa, *First Civil Right*; and Gottschalk, *Prison and the Gallows*.
4. Herrnstein and Murray, *Bell Curve*. A variation of this argument has also been repeated by D'Souza in *The End of Racism*.
5. Lewis and Diamond, *Despite the Best Intentions*.

6. For an elaboration of this subject, see M. Alexander, *New Jim Crow*; and Wacquant, *Prisons of Poverty*.

7. For a study of the way the aftermath of Hurricane Katrina represents the intersections between race, class, and neoliberalism, see Johnson, *Neoliberal Deluge*.

8. For an account of the way black voices are presumptively denigrated and rendered to a condition of anonymity, see Hill, *Nobody*.

9. For an overview of this subject, see the findings of the Michigan Civil Rights Commission, *Flint Water Crisis*.

10. For a scholarly account of this subject, see Hancock, *Politics of Disgust*.

11. For Medicaid enrollment by race, see Henry J. Kaiser Family Foundation, "Distribution of the Nonelderly with Medicaid by Race/Ethnicity." For a history of the way federal social programs have been distributed to assist working-class white people, at the expense of their nonwhite counterparts, see Katznelson, *When Affirmative Action Was White*. For an interpretation of the racialized dimension of why many Americans disapprove of social safety programs, especially welfare, see Gilens, *Why Americans Hate Welfare*.

12. For the classic study of the way whiteness offered a wage for poor white citizens in the United States in prerevolutionary America, see Morgan, *American Slavery, American Freedom*. For an intellectual history of this subject in the nineteenth century, see Du Bois, *Black Reconstruction*; Roediger, *Wages of Whiteness*; and Ignatiev, *How the Irish Became White*.

13. For this argument, see Taylor, *From #BlackLivesMatter to Black Liberation*.

14. For a history of the way white backlash has been integral to impeding black American freedom, see Anderson, *White Rage*. For the critique of "postracialism," see I. Perry, *More Beautiful and More Terrible*. For an interpretation of how postracialism is a myth, despite the election of the first black president, Barack Obama, in 2008, see Tesler and Sears, *Obama's Race*. For federal food-assistance programs, distributed by race (white people make up 40 percent of recipients, whereas black people make up 25 percent, for fiscal year 2015), see United States Department of

Agriculture, "Characteristics of Supplemental Nutrition Assistance Programs."

15. See Jacobsen, *Roots Too*; and Hattam, *In the Shadow of Race*.

16. See Wilson, *When Work Disappears*; and Shelby, *Dark Ghettos*.

17. See Moskowitz, *How to Kill a City*; and Venkatesh, *Gang Leader for a Day*.

18. Lewis and Diamond, *Despite the Best Intentions*; and Massey and Denton, *American Apartheid*.

19. See Human Rights Campaign, "Violence against the Transgender Community in 2018."

20. See Collins and Sirma Bilge, *Intersectionality*; and Hancock, *Intersectionality*.

21. For a recent text that tries to understand the sources and meaning of race rebellions, especially in the 1960s, see Levy, *Great Uprising*.

22. See West, *Race Matters*, chap. 1.

23. This is a general argument of contemporary prison abolitionists who stress the need to dismantle the school-to-prison pipeline and to demilitarize black public spaces and communities. For this argument, see A. Davis, "Meaning of Freedom"; and James, *New Abolitionists*.

24. See Bouie, "Michael Brown Wasn't a Superhuman Demon."

25. For an excellent account of the pervasive anti-blackness in American culture and society see Sharpe, *In the Wake*.

26. Such activists are involved in reconstructing the meaning both of the US public sphere and also of democratic identity—which they envision as subject to revision and remaking. For an argument that democracy is defined through these contestations, see Frank, *Constituent Moments*. For a theoretical argument about the limitations of patriotic politics for racial justice, see Burkey and Zamalin, "Patriotism, Black Politics and Racial Justice in America."

27. A new study finds that black boys who are born into wealthier households are far less likely to be wealthy than are their white counterparts when they reach adult age and are much more likely to live in poverty. See Badger et al., "Extensive Data Shows Punishing Reach of Racism."

28. For an overview of the dominance of this kind of economic policy, otherwise known as "neoliberalism," over the past four decades, see Harvey, *Brief History of Neoliberalism*.
29. As the scholar Erik Love notes, "the racist and demonstrably false stereotype about terrorism and 'Muslims' is so pervasive that openly asserting it has become a perfectly acceptable, mainstream position in the United States" (*Islamophobia and Racism in America*, 7). For an overview of Islamophobia from a legal perspective, see Beydoun, *American Islamophobia*.
30. For a critique of the argument that Islam is a culture of violence, using the cultural hybridity argument—that it is impossible to disentangle the hybridity and borrowing between East and West—see Asad, *On Suicide Bombing*.
31. Though these arguments are central to contemporary feminist arguments, they were most notably made by many second-wave feminists in the 1960s and 1970s. For a representative overview of those writings, see Crow, *Radical Feminism*.
32. For a philosophical argument about the refusal to engage in the denigration of survivors' testimonies, see Alcoff, *Rape and Resistance*.
33. M. Alexander, *New Jim Crow*.
34. For the argument about how language can become a coercive form of power, see Foucault, "Discourse of Language."
35. See Lyman, *Drugs in Society*.
36. Along with direct action strategies, this has been a central rhetorical strategy of "Dreamers," undocumented people who came to the US as children. They argue that their contribution to the economy, and participation in US culture, is a crucial justification for belonging. See Nichols, *DREAMers*.
37. For a recent study of the present and future of Latino politics in the US, with a specific focus on the way Latino protest politics can debate the meaning of democracy, see Beltrán, *Trouble with Unity*.
38. For a recent argument along these lines, see A. Davis, *Freedom Is a Constant Struggle*.
39. Horowitz, Berman, and Lowery, "Sessions Orders Justice Department." Also see Demick and Lee, "Trump Urges Officers and Immigration Officials."

40. Porter, "Prisons Run by CEOs?"

41. Strauss, Douglas-Gabriel, and Balingit, "DeVos Seeks Cuts."

42. For a study of the changing relationship between media and activism, see Gerbaudo, *Tweets and Streets*.

43. Rowland and Eidelman, "Where Protests Flourish."

44. There is a link between black antiracist freedom struggle and what the scholar Jonathan Lear calls "radical hope" (*Radical Hope*).

BIBLIOGRAPHY

Alcoff, Linda Martin. *The Future of Whiteness*. Cambridge, UK: Polity, 2015.

———. *Rape and Resistance*. Cambridge, UK: Polity, 2018.

———. *Visible Identities: Race, Gender, and the Self*. New York: Oxford University Press, 2005.

Alexander, Jeffrey C. *The Civil Sphere*. Oxford: Oxford University Press, 2008.

Alexander, Michelle. *The New Jim Crow: Mass Incarceration in the Age of Colorblindness*. New York: New Press, 2010.

Allen, Danielle. *Talking to Strangers: Anxieties of Citizenship after* Brown v. Board of Education. Chicago: University of Chicago Press, 2004.

Anderson, Carol. *White Rage: The Unspoken Truth of Our Racial Divide*. New York: Bloomsbury, 2017.

Aptheker, Herbert. *American Negro Slave Revolts*. 1943. Reprint, New York: International, 1983.

———. *Anti-Racism in US History: The First 200 Years*. New York: Praeger, 1993.

Asad, Talal. *On Suicide Bombing*. New York: Columbia University Press, 2017.

Asante, Molefi Kete. *Afrocentricity: The Theory of Social Change*. Chicago: African American Images, 2003.

Badger, Emily, Claire Cain Miller, Adam Pearce, and Kevin Quealy. "Extensive Data Shows Punishing Reach of Racism for Black Boys." *New York Times*, March 19, 2018. www.nytimes.com.

Baker, Ella. "Bigger than a Hamburger." *Southern Patriot*, May 1960, 4.

———. "Developing Community Leadership." In *Black Women in White America: A Documentary History*, edited by Gerda Lerner, 351. New York: Pantheon Books, 1972.

Baker, Houston A. *Betrayal: How Black Intellectuals Have Abandoned the Ideals of the Civil Rights Era*. New York: Columbia University Press, 2008.

Baldwin, James. "The American Dream and the American Negro." *New York Times*, March 7, 1965. www.nytimes.com.

———. *The Fire Next Time*. 1963. Reprint, New York: Vintage, 1992.

———. "Many Thousands Gone." In *The Price of the Ticket*, edited by James Baldwin, 65–79. New York: St. Martin's, 1985.

———. "Nobody Knows My Name: Letter from the South." In *The Price of the Ticket*, edited by James Baldwin, 183–194. New York: St. Martin's, 1985.

———. "Stranger in the Village." In *The Price of the Ticket*, edited by James Baldwin, 79–90. New York: St. Martin's, 1985.

———. "We Can Change This Country." 1963. In *Cross of Redemption: Uncollected Writings*, edited by Randall Kenan, 58–64. New York: Vintage, 2010.

———. "White Man's Guilt." In *The Price of the Ticket*, edited by James Baldwin, 409–414. New York: St. Martin's, 1985.

———. "Words of a Native Son." In *The Price of the Ticket*, edited by James Baldwin, 395–402. New York: St. Martin's, 1985.

Balfour, Lawrie. *Democracy's Reconstruction: Thinking Politically with W. E. B. Du Bois*. New York: Oxford University Press, 2011.

Baraka, Amiri. "Confessions of a Former Anti-Semite." *Village Voice*, December 17–23, 1980.

———. "The Pan-African Party and the Black Nation." *Black Scholar* 2, no. 7 (1971): 24–32.

———. *Somebody Blew Up America and Other Poems*. New York: Nehisi, 2014.

Bay, Mia. *To Tell the Truth Freely*. New York: Hill and Wang, 2010.

Bell, Derrick A. *Faces at the Bottom of the Well: The Permanence of Racism*. New York: Basic Books, 1993.

———. "The Unintended Lessons in *Brown v. Board of Education*." *New York Law School Review* 49 (2005): 1053–1067.

Beltrán, Cristina. *The Trouble with Unity: Latino Politics and the Creation of Identity*. New York: Oxford University Press, 2010.

Beydoun, Khaled. *American Islamophobia: Understanding the Roots and Rise of Fear*. Berkeley: University of California Press, 2018.

Black Public Sphere Collective. *The Black Public Sphere*. Chicago: University of Chicago Press, 1995.

Bloom, Waldo E., and Joshua Martin. *Black against Empire: The History and Politics of the Black Panther Party*. Berkeley: University of California Press, 2013.

Bonilla-Silva, Eduardo. *Racism without Racists: Color-Blind Racism and the Persistence of Racial Inequality in America*. Lanham, MD: Rowman and Littlefield, 2017.

Bouie, Jamelle. "Michael Brown Wasn't a Superhuman Demon." *Slate*, November 26, 2014. www.slate.com.

Bromell, Nick. *The Time Is Always Now: Black Thought and the Transformation of US Democracy*. New York: Oxford University Press, 2013.

Bronner, Stephen Eric. *Reclaiming the Enlightenment: Toward a Politics of Radical Engagement*. New York: Columbia University Press, 2004.

Brown, Elaine. *A Taste of Power: A Black Woman's Story*. New York: Random House, 1992.

Burkey, Maxwell, and Alex Zamalin. "Patriotism, Black Politics and Racial Justice in America." *New Political Science* 38, no. 3 (2016): 371–389.

Calhoun, John C. "Speech on the Reception of Abolition Petitions, Delivered in the Senate, February 6th, 1837." In *Speeches of John C. Calhoun, Delivered in the House of Representatives and in the Senate of the United States*, edited by Richard R. Crallé, 625–633. New York: D. Appleton, 1853.

Campbell, James. "Revolution Song." *Guardian*, August 3, 2007. www.theguardian.com.

Carmichael, Stokely. "Berkeley Speech." In *Stokely Speaks*, 45–60. Chicago: Chicago Review Press, 2007.

———. *Ready for Revolution: The Life and Times of Stokely Carmichael (Kwame Ture)*. New York: Scribner, 2005.

Carson, Clayborne. *In Struggle: SNCC and the Black Awakening of the 1960s*. Cambridge, MA: Harvard University Press, 1981.

Coates, Ta-Nehisi. *Between the World and Me*. New York: Spiegel and Grau, 2015.

Collins, Patricia Hill. *Black Feminist Thought*. New York: Routledge, 1990.

Collins, Patricia Hill, and Sirma Bilge. *Intersectionality*. New York: Oxford University Press, 2016.

Combahee River Collective. "A Black Feminist Statement." In *The Bridge Called My Back: Writings by Radical Women of Color*, edited by Cherríe Moraga and Gloria Anzaldúa, 210–219. New York: SUNY Press, 2015.

Cone, James. *A Black Theology of Liberation*. Maryknoll, NY: Orbis Books, 2010.

Cooper, Anna Julia. *A Voice from the South*. 1892. Reprint, New York: Dover, 2016.

Crenshaw, Kimberlé Williams. "Mapping the Margins: Intersectionality, Identity Politics, and Violence against Women of Color." *Stanford Law Review* 43, no. 6 (1991): 1241–1299.

Crow, Barbara A., ed. *Radical Feminism: A Documentary Reader*. New York: NYU Press, 2000.

Davis, Angela. *Freedom Is a Constant Struggle: Ferguson, Palestine, and the Foundations of a Movement*. Chicago: Haymarket Books, 2016.

———. "The Meaning of Freedom." In *The Meaning of Freedom*, edited by Angela Davis, 135–152. New York: Seven Stories, 2012.

———. "The Prison-Industrial Complex." In *The Meaning of Freedom*, edited by Angela Davis, 35–54. New York: Seven Stories, 2012.

———. *Women, Race, and Class*. New York: Vintage, 1983.

Davis, David Brion. *Slavery and Human Progress*. New York: Oxford University Press, 1986.

Davis, Ossie. "Eulogy of Malcolm X." In *SOS—Calling All Black People: A Black Arts Movement Reader*, edited by John H. Bracey Jr., Sonia Sanchez, and James Smethurst, 310. Amherst: University of Massachusetts Press, 2014.

Dawson, Michael C. *Behind the Mule: Race and Class in African-American Politics*. Princeton, NJ: Princeton University Press, 1995.

———. *Black Visions: The Roots of Contemporary African-American Political Ideologies*. Chicago: University of Chicago Press, 2001.

Delany, Martin. *The Condition, Elevation, Emigration and Destiny of the Colored People*. 1852. Reprint, Philadelphia: Black Classic, 1993.

Delgado, Richard, and Jean Stefancic. *Critical Race Theory: An Introduction*. New York: NYU Press, 2012.

Demick, Barbara, and Kurtis Lee. "Trump Urges Officers and Immigration Officials to Be 'Rough' on 'Animals' Terrorizing U.S. Neighborhoods." *Los Angeles Times*, July 28, 2017. www.latimes.com.

Douglass, Frederick. *The Autobiographies*. New York: Library of America, 1994.

———. "The Constitution of the United States: Is It Pro-Slavery or Anti-Slavery?" In *Frederick Douglass: Selected Speeches and Writings*, edited by Philip S. Foner and Yuval Taylor, 379–390. Chicago: Lawrence Hill Books, 1999.

———. "The Meaning of July Fourth for the Negro." In *Frederick Douglass: Selected Speeches and Writings*, edited by Philip S. Foner and Yuval Taylor, 188–205. Chicago: Lawrence Hill Books, 1999.

D'Souza Dinesh. *The End of Racism: Principles for a Multiracial Society*. New York: Free Press, 1995.

———. *The Roots of Obama's Rage*. Washington, DC: Regnery, 2010.

Du Bois, W. E. B. *Black Reconstruction in America*. 1935. New York: Atheneum, 1992.

———. *Darkwater: Voices from Within the Well*. New York: Harcourt, Brace, and Howe, 1920.

———. *The Gift of Black Folk: The Negroes in the Making of America*. New York: Stratford, 1924.

———. *The Philadelphia Negro*. Philadelphia: University of Pennsylvania Press, 1899.

———. *The Souls of Black Folk*. 1903. Reprint, New York: Oxford University Press, 2007.

Dudziak, Mary. *Cold War Civil Rights: Race and the Image of American Democracy*. Princeton, NJ: Princeton University Press, 2001.

Dunbar, Paul Laurence. "Sympathy." In *The Collected Poetry of Paul Lawrence Dunbar*, edited by Joanne M. Braxton, 102. Charlottesville: University of Virginia Press, 1993.

Ellison, Ralph. "*An American Dilemma*: A Review." In *The Collected Essays of Ralph Ellison*, edited by John Callahan, 328–340. New York: Modern Library, 1995.

———. "An Extravagance of Laughter." 1985. In *The Collected Essays of Ralph Ellison*, edited by John Callahan, 617–662. New York: Modern Library, 1995.

———. *Invisible Man*. 1952. Reprint, New York: Vintage, 1995.

———. "The Little Man at Chehaw Station." In *The Collected Essays of Ralph Ellison*, edited by John Callahan, 493–524. New York: Modern Library, 1995.

Emery, Kathy, Sylvia Braselmann, and Linda Reid Gold. "Introduction: Freedom Summer and the Freedom Schools." In *Freedom School Curriculum*. Education & Democracy website. http://educationand-democracy.org.

Fanon, Frantz. *Wretched of the Earth*. New York: Grove, 1995.

Ferguson, Jeffrey. *The Sage of Sugar Hill: George S. Schuyler and the Harlem Renaissance*. New Haven, CT: Yale University Press, 2005.

Fields, Karen E., and Barbara Fields. *Racecraft: The Soul of Inequality in American Life*. New York: Verso, 2014.

Foner, Eric. *The Gateway to Freedom: The Hidden History of the Underground Railroad*. New York: Norton, 2016.

———. *Reconstruction, 1863–1877*. New York: Harper and Row, 1988.

Forman, James. "Black Manifesto." *New York Review*, July 10, 1969. www.nybooks.com.

Fortune, T. Thomas. *Black and White: Land, Labor, and Politics in the South*. 1883. Reprint, New York: Simon and Schuster, 2007.

Foucault, Michel. "The Discourse of Language." In *The Archeology of Knowledge*, 215–238. New York: Vintage, 1982.

Frank, Jason. *Constituent Moments: Enacting the People in Postrevolutionary America*. Durham, NC: Duke University Press, 2009.

Fredrickson, George. *Black Liberation: A Comparative Study of Liberation Ideologies in the United States and South Africa*. New York: Oxford University Press, 1996.

———. *Racism: A Short History*. Princeton, NJ: Princeton University Press, 2009.

Freeden, Michael. *Liberalism: A Very Short Introduction*. New York: Oxford University Press 2015.

Gaines, Kevin. *Uplifting the Race: Black Leadership, Politics, and Culture in the Twentieth Century*. Chapel Hill: University of North Carolina Press, 1996.

Garnet, Henry Highland. "An Address to the Slaves of the United States of America" (1843). *Electronic Texts in American Studies* 8. Digital Commons, University of Nebraska–Lincoln. https://digitalcommons.unl.edu.

Genovese, Eugene. *From Rebellion to Revolution: Afro-American Slave Revolts in the Making of the Modern World*. Baton Rouge: Louisiana State University Press, 1992.

Gerbaudo, Paolo. *Tweets and Streets: Social Media and Contemporary Activism*. New York: Pluto, 2012.

Gilens, Martin. *Why Americans Hate Welfare: Race, Media, and the Politics of Antipoverty Policy*. Chicago: University of Chicago Press, 2000.

Gilroy, Paul. *Against Race: Imagining Political Culture beyond the Color Line*. Cambridge, MA: Harvard University Press, 2000.

Glaude, Eddie, Jr. *Exodus! Religion, Race and Nation in Early Nineteenth-Century Black America*. Chicago: University of Chicago Press, 2000.

Gooding-Williams, Robert. *In the Shadow of Du Bois: Afro-Modern Political Thought in America*. Cambridge, MA: Harvard University Press, 2011.

Gordon, Jane Anna. *Creolizing Political Theory: Reading Rousseau through Fanon*. New York: Fordham University Press, 2014.

Gordon, Jane Anna, and Neil Roberts, eds. *Creolizing Rousseau*. Lanham, MD: Rowman and Littlefield, 2014.

Gordon, Lewis R. *Bad Faith and Antiblack Racism*. Amherst, NY: Humanity Books, 1995.

———. *An Introduction to Africana Philosophy*. New York: Cambridge University Press, 2008.

Gottschalk, Marie. *The Prison and the Gallows: The Politics of Mass Incarceration in America*. New York: Cambridge University Press, 2006.

Hall, Jacqueline Dowd. "The Long Civil Rights Movement and the Political Uses of the Past." *Journal of America History* 91, no. 4 (2005): 1233–1263.

Hamer, Fannie Lou. *The Speeches of Fannie Lou Hamer: To Tell It Like It Is*. Edited by Meagan Parker Brooks and Davis W. Houck. Oxford: University Press of Mississippi, 2013.

Hamilton, Charles, and Kwame Ture. *Black Power: The Politics of Liberation in America*. New York: Random House, 1967.

Hancock, Ange-Marie. *Intersectionality: An Intellectual History*. New York: Oxford University Press, 2017.

———. *The Politics of Disgust: The Public Identity of the Welfare Queen*. New York: NYU Press, 2004.

Hartz, Louis. *The Liberal Tradition in America: An Interpretation of American Political Thought since the Revolution*. New York: Harcourt, Brace, and Jovanovich, 1991.

Harvey, David. *A Brief History of Neoliberalism*. New York: Oxford University Press, 2007.

Hattam, Victoria. *In the Shadow of Race: Jews, Latinos, and Immigrant Politics in the United States*. Chicago: University of Chicago Press, 2007.

Hawley, George. *Making Sense of the Alt-Right*. New York: Columbia University Press, 2017.

Henry, Paget. *Caliban's Reason: Introducing Afro-Caribbean Philosophy*. New York: Routledge, 2000.

Henry J. Kaiser Family Foundation. "Distribution of the Nonelderly with Medicaid by Race/Ethnicity, 2016." Accessed April 15, 2017. www.kff.org.

Herrnstein, Richard J., and Charles Murray. *The Bell Curve: Intelligence and Class Structure in American Life*. New York: Free Press, 1996.

Hill, Marc Lamont. *Nobody: Causalities of America's War on the Vulnerable, from Ferguson to Flint and Beyond*. New York: Atria, 2015.

Hofstadter, Richard. *The American Political Tradition: And the Men Who Made It*. New York: Vintage, 1989.

Holiday, Billie. "Strange Fruit." Written by Abel Meeropol. *Fine and Mellow*. Commodore Records, 1939.

Hooker, Juliet. *Theorizing Race in the Americas: Douglass, Sarmiento, Du Bois, and Vasconcelos*. New York: Oxford University Press, 2017.

hooks, bell. *Ain't I a Woman?* New York: Pluto, 1982.

Horowitz, Sari, Mark Berman, and Wesley Lower. "Sessions Orders Justice Department to Review All Police Reform Agreements." *Washington Post*, April 3, 2017. www.washingtonpost.com.

Hughes, Langston. "Let America Be America Again." 1938. In *The Collected Poems of Langston Hughes*, edited by Arnold Rampersad, 190–193. New York: Knopf, 1994.

Human Rights Campaign. "Violence against the Transgender Community in 2018." Accessed April 7, 2018.

Ignatiev, Noel. *How the Irish Became White*. New York: Routledge, 2008.

Isaac, Benjamin. *The Invention of Racism in Classical Antiquity*. Princeton, NJ: Princeton University Press, 2006.

Iton, Richard. *In Search of the Black Fantastic: Politics and Popular Culture in the Post–Civil Rights Era*. New York: Oxford University Press, 2011.

Jackson, Walter A. *Gunnar Myrdal and America's Conscience: Social Engineering and Racial Liberalism, 1938–1987*. Chapel Hill: University of North Carolina Press, 1990.

Jacobs, Harriet Ann. *Incidents in the Life of a Slave Girl*. 1861. Reprint, New York: Dover, 2001.

Jacobsen, Matthew Frye. *Roots Too: White Ethnic Revival in Post–Civil Rights America*. Cambridge, MA: Harvard University Press, 2008.

———. *Whiteness of a Different Color: European Immigrants and the Alchemy of Race*. Cambridge, MA: Harvard University Press, 1998.

Jacobson, Roni. "Claudette Colvin Explains Her Role in the Civil Rights Movement." *Teen Vogue*, October 19, 2017. www.teenvogue.com.

James, Joy, ed. *The New Abolitionists: (Neo)Slave Narratives and Contemporary Prison Writings*. Albany: SUNY Press, 2005.

James, Joy, and T. Denean Sharpley-Whiting, eds. *The Black Feminist Reader*. London: Wiley-Blackwell, 2000.

Jefferson, Thomas. *Notes on the State of Virginia*. Boston: Lily and Wait, 1781.

Jeffries, Judson. *Huey P. Newton: The Radical Theorist*. Oxford: University of Mississippi Press, 2002.

Johnson, Cedric, ed. *The Neoliberal Deluge: Hurricane Katrina, Late Capitalism, and the Remaking of New Orleans*. Minneapolis: University of Minnesota Press, 2011.

Jones, LeRoi. *Blues People: Negro Music in White America*. 1963. Reprint, New York: Harper Perennial, 1992.

———. *Dutchman*. 1964. In *"Dutchman" and "The Slave": Two Plays*, 1–38. New York: Harper Perennial, 1971.

Katznelson, Ira. *When Affirmative Action Was White: An Untold History of Racial Inequality in Twentieth-Century America*. New York: Norton, 2005.

Kelley, Robin D. G. *Hammer and Hoe: Alabama Communists during the Great Depression*. Chapel Hill: University Press of North Carolina, 2015.

———. *Yo' Mama's Disfunktional! Fighting the Culture Wars in Urban America*. Boston: Beacon, 1998.

Kellogg, Charles Flint. *NAACP: A History of the National Association for the Advancement of Colored People*. Baltimore: Johns Hopkins University Press, 1973.

Kendi, Ibram X. *Stamped from the Beginning: The Definitive History of Racist Ideas in America*. New York: Nation Books, 2016.

Keyssar, Alexander. *The Right to Vote: The Contested History of Democracy in the United States*. New York: Basic Books, 2000.

King, Desmond S., and Rogers Smith. *Still a House Divided: Race and Politics in Obama's America*. Princeton, NJ: Princeton University Press, 2013.

King, Martin Luther, Jr. "The Case against 'Tokenism.'" 1962. In *A Testament of Hope*, edited by James M. Washington, 106–111. New York: HarperCollins, 1986.

———. "An Experiment in Love." In *A Testament of Hope*, edited by James M. Washington, 16–20. New York: HarperCollins, 1986.

———. "I Have a Dream." 1963. In *A Testament of Hope*, edited by James M. Washington, 217–220. New York: HarperCollins, 1986.

———. "Letter from Birmingham City Jail." 1963. In *A Testament of Hope*, edited by James M. Washington, 289–302. New York: HarperCollins, 1986.

———. "Love, Law, and Civil Disobedience." 1961. In *A Testament of Hope*, edited by James M. Washington, 43–53. New York: HarperCollins, 1986.

———. "*Playboy* Interview." 1965. In *A Testament of Hope*, edited by James M. Washington, 340–376. New York: HarperCollins, 1986.

———. "The Rising Tide of Racial Consciousness." 1960. In *A Testament of Hope*, edited by James M. Washington, 145–151. New York: Harper-Collins, 1986.

———. "A Time to Break Silence." 1967. In *A Testament of Hope*, edited by James M. Washington, 231–244. New York: HarperCollins, 1986.

Klein, Naomi. *No Is Not Enough: Resisting Trump's Shock Politics and Winning the World We Need*. Chicago: Haymarket Books, 2017.

Kloppenberg, James T. *Reading Obama: Dreams, Hope, and the American Political Tradition*. Princeton, NJ: Princeton University Press, 2010.

———. *Uncertain Victory: Social Democracy and Progressivism in European and American Thought, 1870–1920*. New York: Oxford University Press, 1988.

Kolchin, Peter. *American Slavery: 1619–1877*. New York: Hill and Wang, 2003.

Larsen, Nella. *Passing*. New York: Knopf, 1929.

Lear, Jonathan. *Radical Hope: Ethics in the Face of Cultural Devastation*. Cambridge, MA: Harvard University Press, 2008.

Lebron, Christopher. *Black Lives Matter: The Making of an Idea*. New York: Oxford University Press, 2017.

Levy, Peter. *The Great Uprising: Race Riots in Urban America during the 1960s*. Cambridge: Cambridge University Press, 2018.

Lewis, Amanda E., and John B. Diamond. *Despite the Best Intentions: How Racial Inequality Thrives in Good Schools*. New York: Oxford University Press, 2015.

Lewis, David Levering. *W. E. B Du Bois: A Biography, 1868–1963*. New York: Holt, 2009.

Lieberman, Robert C. *Shaping Race Policy: The United States in Comparative Perspective*. Princeton, NJ: Princeton University Press, 2007.

———. *Shifting the Color Line: Race and the American Welfare State*. Cambridge, MA: Harvard University Press, 1998.

Lilla, Mark. *The Shipwrecked Mind: On Political Reaction*. New York: New York Review of Books, 2016.

Litwack, Leon. *Trouble in Mind: Black Southerners in the Age of Jim Crow*. New York: Vintage, 1998.

Locke, Alain. "The New Negro." In *The New Negro*, edited by Alain Locke, 3–16. 1925. Reprint, New York: Simon and Shuster, 1992.

Locke, John. *Second Treatise of Government*. Edited by C. B. Macpherson. Indianapolis: Hackett, 1980.

Lorde, Audre. "Age, Race, Class, and Sex: Women Redefining Difference." In *Sister/Outsider: Essays and Speeches*, edited by Audre Lorde, 114–123. Berkeley, CA: Crossing, 1984.

———. "The Master's Tools Will Never Dismantle the Master's House." In *Sister/Outsider*, 110–113. Berkeley, CA: Crossing, 1984.

———. "Scratching the Surface: Some Notes on Barriers to Women and Loving." In *Sister/Outsider: Essays and Speeches*, edited by Audre Lorde, 45–52. Berkeley, CA: Crossing, 1984.

———, ed. *Sister/Outsider: Essays and Speeches*. Berkeley, CA: Crossing, 1984.

———. "There Is No Hierarchy of Oppression." In *I Am Your Sister: Collected and Unpublished Writings of Audre Lorde*, edited by Rudolph P. Byrd, Johnnetta Betsch Cole, and Beverly Guy-Sheftall, 219–221. New York: Oxford University Press, 2011.

———. "Uses of the Erotic: The Erotic as Power." In *Sister/Outsider: Essays and Speeches*, edited by Audre Lorde, 53–59. Berkeley, CA: Crossing, 1984.

Love, Erik. *Islamophobia and Racism in America*. New York: NYU Press, 2017.

Lowery, Wesley. *They Can't Kill Us All: Ferguson, Baltimore, and a New Era in America's Racial Justice Movement*. New York: Little, Brown, 2016.

Lowndes, Joseph. *From the New Deal to the New Right: Race and the Making of Modern Conservatism*. New Haven, CT: Yale University Press, 2008.

Luders, Joseph. *The Civil Rights Movement and the Logic of Social Change*. Cambridge: Cambridge University Press, 2010.

Lyman, Michael D. *Drugs in Society: Causes, Concepts, and Control*. New York: Routledge, 2016.

Malcolm X. "America's Gravest Crisis since the Civil War." Speech at University of California, Berkeley, October 11, 1963. In *Malcolm X: The Last Speeches*, edited by Bruce Perry, 59–79. New York: Pathfinder, 1989.

———. "The Bullet or the Ballot." In *Selected Speeches and Statements*, edited by George Breitman, 23–44. New York: Grove, 1967.

———. *By Any Means Necessary*. New York: Pathfinder, 1992.

———. Letter to the editor. *Egyptian Gazette*, August 25, 1964.

———. "Not Just an American Problem, but a World Problem." Speech, February 16, 1965. In *Malcolm X: The Last Speeches*, edited by Bruce Perry, 153–184. New York: Pathfinder, 1989.

———. Roundtable with Malcolm X, James Farmer, Wyatt T. Walker, and Alan Morrison. *Open Mind*, PBS, aired October 5, 1961. Accessed April 7, 2018. www.youtube.com.

Malcolm X and Alex Haley. *The Autobiography of Malcolm X: As Told to Alex Haley*. New York: Ballantine Books, 1964.

Mantler, Gordon K. *Power to the Poor: Black-Brown Coalition and the Fight for Economic Justice, 1960–1974*. Chapel Hill: University of North Carolina Press, 2015.

Marable, Manning. *Malcolm X: A Life of Reinvention*. New York: Penguin Books, 2011.

———. *Race, Rebellion, and Reform: The Second Reconstruction and Beyond in Black America*. Oxford: University Press of Mississippi, 2007.

Marshall, Stephen. *The City on the Hill from Below: The Crisis of Prophetic Black Politics*. Philadelphia: Temple University Press, 2011.

Martin, Waldo E. *The Mind of Frederick Douglass*. Chapel Hill: University of North Carolina Press, 1984.

Massey, Douglas S., and Nancy A. Denton. *American Apartheid: Segregation and the Making of the Underclass*. Cambridge, MA: Harvard University Press, 1993.

McAdam, Doug. *Political Process and the Development of Black Insurgency, 1930–1970*. Chicago: University of Chicago Press.

McKnight, Utz. *The Everyday Practice of Race in America: Ambiguous Privilege*. New York: Routledge, 2010.

———. *Race and the Politics of Exception: Equality, Sovereignty and American Democracy*. New York: Routledge, 2013.

McWhorter, John. *Winning the Race: Beyond the Crisis in Black America*. New York: Gotham, 2005.

Mehta, Uday S. *Liberalism and Empire: A Study in Nineteenth-Century British Liberal Thought*. Chicago: University of Chicago Press, 1999.

Memmi, Albert. *Racism*. Minneapolis: University of Minnesota Press, 1999.

"Meredith Appears in Ad for David Duke." *Star News*, October 13, 1991.

Michigan Civil Rights Commission. *The Flint Water Crisis: Systemic Racism through the Lens of Flint*. February 17, 2017. www.michigan.gov.

Mills, Charles W. *Black Rights / White Wrongs: The Critique of Racial Liberalism*. New York: Oxford University Press, 2017.

———. *From Class to Race: Essays on White Marxism and Black Radicalism*. Lanham, MD: Rowman and Littlefield, 2003.

———. *The Racial Contract*. Ithaca, NY: Cornell University Press, 1997.

Morgan, Edmund S. *American Slavery, American Freedom*. New York: Norton, 1975.

Morris, Aldon. *The Origins of the Civil Rights Movement: Black Communities Organizing for Change*. New York: Free Press, 1986.

Morrison, Toni. *Beloved*. New York: Knopf, 1987.

———. *Paradise*. New York: Knopf, 1997.

Moses, Robert P., and Charles Cobb. *Radical Equations: Civil Rights from Mississippi to the Algebra Project*. Boston: Beacon, 2002.

Moses, Wilson J. *The Golden Age of Black Nationalism: 1850–1925*. New York: Oxford University Press, 1988.

Moskowitz, Peter. *How to Kill a City: Gentrification, Inequality, and the Fight for the Neighborhood*. New York: Nation Books, 2017.

Moten, Fred. *In the Break: The Aesthetics of the Black Radical Tradition*. Minneapolis: University of Minnesota Press, 2003.

Mouffe, Chantal. *The Democratic Paradox*. New York: Verso, 2000.

Movement for Black Lives. "Platform." Accessed August 15, 2017. https://policy.m4bl.org.

Murakawa, Naomi. *The First Civil Right: How Liberals Built Prison America*. New York: Oxford University Press, 2014.

Myrdal, Gunnar. *An American Dilemma*. New York: Harper and Row, 1944.

National Advisory Commission on Civil Disorders. *The Kerner Report*. Princeton, NJ: Princeton University Press, 2016.

Nelson, Crystal, Caty Thomas, and Kiran Garcha. "Liberation Schools." *Scalar*, February 7, 2017. http://scalar.usc.edu.

Newton, Huey P. "Intercommunalism." In *The Huey P. Newton Reader*, edited by David Hilliard, 181–199. New York: Seven Stories, 2002.

———. "The Women's Liberation and Gay Liberation Movements." In *The Huey P. Newton Reader*, edited by David Hilliard, 157–159. New York: Seven Stories, 2002.

Nichols, Walter J. *The DREAMers: How the Undocumented Youth Movement Transformed the Immigrant Rights Debate*. Stanford, CA: Stanford University Press, 2013.

Norton, Anne. *95 Theses on Politics, Culture, and Method*. New Haven, CT: Yale University Press, 2004.

Obama, Barack. "Barack Obama's Speech on Race." *New York Times*, March 18, 2008. www.nytimes.com.

Oliver, Melvin L., and Thomas M. Shapiro. *Black Wealth, White Wealth: A New Perspective on Racial Inequality*. London: Routledge, 2006.

Omi, Michael, and Howard Winant. *Racial Formation in the United States*. New York: Routledge, 1994.

Payne, Charles M. *I've Got the Light of Freedom: The Organizing Tradition and the Mississippi Freedom Struggle*. Berkeley: University of California Press, 1995.

Perry, Imani. *More Beautiful and More Terrible: The Embrace and Transcendence of Racial Inequality in America*. New York: NYU Press, 2011.

Perry, Jeffrey B. *Hubert Harrison: The Voice of Harlem Radicalism, 1883–1928*. New York: Columbia University Press, 2009.

Piven, Frances Fox, and Richard Cloward. *Poor People's Movements: Why They Succeed, How They Fail*. New York: Vintage, 1978.

Porter, Eduardo. "Prisons Run by CEOs? Privatization under Trump Could Carry a Heavy Price." *New York Times*, January 10, 2017, www.nytimes.com.

Prison Research Education Action Project. *Instead of Prisons: A Handbook for Abolitionists*. Oakland, CA: Critical Resistance, 2001.

Randolph, A. Philip. "Address at the March on Washington for Jobs and Freedom." In *For Jobs and Freedom: Selected Speeches and Writings of A. Philip Randolph*, edited by Andrew Kersten and David Lucander, 261–263. Amherst: University of Massachusetts Press, 2014.

Rattansi, Ali. *Racism: A Very Short Introduction*. New York: Oxford University Press, 2007.

Rawley, Hazel. *Richard Wright: The Life and Times*. Chicago: University of Chicago Press, 2001.

Rawls, John. *A Theory of Justice*. Cambridge, MA: Harvard University Press, 1971.

Reed, Adolph. *Class Notes: Posing as Politics and Other Notes on the Class Scene*. New York: New Press, 2001.

Roberts, Neil. *Freedom as Marronage*. Chicago: University of Chicago Press, 2015.

Robin, Corey. *The Reactionary Mind: From Edmund Burke to Donald Trump*. New York: Oxford University Press, 2017.

Robinson, Cedric J. *Black Marxism: The Making of the Black Radical Tradition*. 1983. Reprint, Chapel Hill: University of North Carolina Press, 2000.

Robinson, Dean E. *Black Nationalism in American Political and Thought*. Cambridge: Cambridge University Press, 2001.

Robinson, Randall. *The Debt: What America Owes to Blacks*. New York: Plume, 2001.

Roediger, David R. *The Wages of Whiteness: Race and the Making of the American Working Class*. New York: Verso, 1999.

Rogin, Michael. *Fathers and Children: Andrew Jackson and the Subjugation of the American Indian*. New York: Routledge, 1991.

Rowland, Lee, and Vera Eidelman, "Where Protests Flourish, Anti-Protest Bills Follow." *Speak Freely* (blog), ACLU, February 17, 2017. www.aclu.org.

Rustin, Bayard. "From Protest to Politics: The Future of the Civil Rights Movement." 1964. In *Time on Two Crosses: The Collected Writings of Bayard Rustin*, edited by Devon Carbado and Don Weise, 116–129. New York: Cleis, 2004.

Sartre, Jean-Paul. *Anti-Semite and Jew: An Exploration of the Etiology of Hate*. New York: Schocken, 1995.

Schuyler, George S. *Black No More: Being an Account of Strange and Wonderful Workings of Science in the Land of the Free, A.D. 1933–1940*. 1931. Reprint, New York: Modern Library, 1999.

Scott, Daryl Michael. *Contempt and Pity: Social Policy and the Image of the Damage Black Psyche, 1880–1996*. Chapel Hill: University of North Carolina Press, 1997.

Sharpe, Christina. *In the Wake: On Blackness and Being*. Durham, NC: Duke University Press, 2015.

Shelby, Tommie. *Dark Ghettos: Injustice, Dissent, Reform*. Cambridge, MA: Harvard University Press, 2016.

Simone, Nina. "I Wish I Knew How It Feels to Be Free." *Silk & Soul*. RCA Records, 1967.

———. "Mississippi Goddam." *Nina Simone in Concert*. Philips Records, 1964.

Smith, Andrea. *Conquest: Sexual Violence and American Indian Genocide*. Durham, NC: Duke University Press, 2015.

Southern Poverty Law Center. *Intelligence Report* 162 (Spring 2017). www.splcenter.org.

Stack, Liam. "Ben Carson Refers to Slaves as 'Immigrants' in First Remarks to HUD Staff." *New York Times*, March 17, 2017.

Steele, Shelby. *Shame: How America's Past Sins Have Polarized Our Country*. New York: Basic Books, 2015.

Stein, Judith. *Marcus Garvey: Race and Class in Modern Society*. Baton Rouge: Louisiana State University Press, 1991.

Steinberg, Stephen. *Turning Back: The Retreat from Racial Justice in American Thought and Policy*. Boston: Beacon, 2001.

Stetson, Erlene, and Linda David. *Glorying in Tribulation: The Lifework of Sojourner Truth*. Ann Arbor: University of Michigan Press, 1994.

Stevens, Margaret. *Red International and Black Caribbean: Communists in New York City, Mexico and the West Indies, 1913–1939*. New York: Pluto, 2017.

Stewart, Maria. "An Address Delivered at the African Masonic Hall, Boston, 1833." In *Maria W. Stewart: America's First Black Woman Political Writer*, edited by Marilyn Richardson, 56–64. Bloomington: Indiana University Press, 1987.

———. "Lecture Delivered at Franklin Hall." In *Maria W. Stewart: America's First Black Woman Political Writer*, edited by Marilyn Richardson, 45–49. Bloomington: Indiana University Press, 1987.

Strauss, Valerie, Danielle Douglas-Gabriel, and Moriah Balingit. "DeVos Seeks Cuts from Education Department to Support School Choice." *Washington Post*, February 13, 2018. www.washingtonpost.com.

Stuckey, Sterling. *The Ideological Origins of Black Nationalism*. Boston: Beacon, 1972.

Sumner, William Graham. *What Social Classes Owe to Each Other*. New Haven, CT: Yale University Press, 1925.

Sun Ra. *The Immeasurable Equation: The Collected Poetry and Prose*, edited by James L. Wolf and Hartmut Geerken. Chandler, AZ: Phaelos Books, 2005.

Taylor, Keeanga-Yamahtta. *From #BlackLivesMatter to Black Liberation*. Chicago: Haymarket Books, 2015.

Tesler, Michael, and David O. Sears. *Obama's Race: The 2008 Election and the Dream of a Post-Racial America*. Chicago: University of Chicago Press, 2010.

Threadcraft, Shatema. *Intimate Justice: The Black Female Body and the Body Politic*. New York: Oxford University Press, 2016.

Thrush, Glenn. "Under Ben Carson, HUD Scales Back Fair Housing Enforcement." *New York Times*, March 28, 2018.

Trend, David, ed. *Radical Democracy: Identity, Citizenship and the State*. New York: Routledge, 2013.

Trump, Donald. "Full Text: Trump's Comments on White Supremacists, 'Alt-Left' in Charlottesville." *Politico*, August 15, 2017. www.politico.com.

Ture, Kwame. "Berkeley Speech." In *Stokely Speaks: From Black Power to Black Nationalism*, edited by Kwame Ture, 45–60. Chicago: Chicago Review Press, 2007.

Ture, Kwame, and Charles V. Hamilton. *Black Power: The Politics of Liberation*. New York: Vintage, 1992.

Turner, Jack. *Awakening to Race: Individualism and Social Consciousness in America*. Chicago: University of Chicago Press, 2012.

United States Department of Agriculture. "Characteristics of Supplemental Nutrition Assistance Households: Fiscal Year 2015." January 17, 2018. www.fns.usda.gov.

Venkatesh, Sudhir. *Gang Leader for a Day: A Rogue Sociologist Takes to the Streets*. New York: Penguin Books, 2008.

Wacquant, Loïc. *Prisons of Poverty*. Minneapolis: University of Minnesota Press, 2009.

Waldrep, Christopher. *African Americans Confront Lynching: Strategies of Resistance from the Civil War to the Civil Rights Era*. Lanham, MD: Rowman and Littlefield, 2009.

Walker, David. *Appeal in Four Articles; Together with a Preamble, to the Coloured Citizens of the World, but in Particular, and Very Expressly, to Those of the United States of America*. 1829. Accessed August 5, 1017. University Library of the University of North Carolina–Chapel Hill, *Documenting the American South*. http://docsouth.unc.edu.

Washington, Booker T. "The Standard Printed Version of the Atlanta Exposition Address." 1895. In *The Booker T. Washington Papers*, edited by Louis R. Harlan, 583–588. Urbana: University of Illinois Press, 1971.

Washington, Mary Helen. *Invented Lives: Narratives of Black Women, 1860–1960*. New York: Anchor, 1987.

Watts, Jerry Gafio. *Amiri Baraka: The Politics and Art of a Black Intellectual*. New York: NYU Press, 2001.

Wells, Ida B. "Ida B. Wells Case." A legal brief for Wells's lawsuit against Chesapeake, Ohio, and Southwestern Railroad Company before the state supreme court, 1885. Digital Public Library of America. http://dp.la.

———. "Lynch Law in America." 1900. In *The Light of Truth: Writings of an Anti-Lynching Crusader*, edited by Mia Bay, 394–403. New York: Penguin Books, 2014.

———. *A Red Record*. 1895. In *The Light of Truth: Writings of an Anti-Lynching Crusader*, edited by Mia Bay, 218–312. New York: Penguin Books, 2014.

——. *Southern Horrors: Lynch Law in All Its Phases*, 57–82. 1892. In *The Light of Truth: Writings of an Anti-Lynching Crusader*, edited by Mia Bay. New York: Penguin Books, 2014.

West, Cornel. "Black Strivings in a Twilight Civilization." In *The Cornel West Reader*, edited by Cornel West, 87–118. New York: BasicCivitas Books, 1999.

——. *Prophesy Deliverance! An Afro-American Revolutionary Christianity*. Louisville, KY: Westminster John Knox Press, 2002.

——. *Race Matters*. Boston: Beacon, 2001.

Wilson, William Julius. *More than Just Race: Being Black and Poor in the Inner City*. New York: Norton, 2010.

——. *When Work Disappears: The World of the New Urban Poor*. New York: Vintage, 1997.

Winders, Bill. "New Deal Agricultural Policy: The Unintended Consequences of Supply Management." In *When Government Helped: Learning from the Successes and Failures of the New Deal*, edited by Sheila Collins and Gertrude Shafner Goldberg, 266–291. New York: Oxford University Press, 2014.

Winter, Jana, and Sharon Weinberger. "The FBI's New U.S. Terrorist Threat: 'Black Identity Extremists.'" *Foreign Policy*, October 6, 2017.

Winters, Joseph R. *Hope Draped in Black: Race, Melancholy, and the Agony of Racial Progress*. Durham, NC: Duke University Press, 2016.

Wolin, Sheldon. *Politics and Vision: Continuity and Innovation in Western Political Thought*. Princeton, NJ: Princeton University Press, 2004.

Wright, Richard. "Blueprint for Negro Writing." In *The Portable Harlem Renaissance Reader*, edited by David Levering Lewis, 194–205. New York: Viking, 1994.

——. *Native Son*. New York: Harper, 1940.

Zamalin, Alex. *Struggle on Their Minds: The Political Thought of African American Resistance*. New York: Columbia University Press, 2017.

INDEX

ABOUT THE AUTHOR

Alex Zamalin is Assistant Professor of Political Science and Director of African American Studies at the University of Detroit Mercy. He is the author of *African American Political Thought and American Culture: The Nation's Struggle for Racial Justice* (2015) and *Struggle on Their Minds: The Political Thought of African American Resistance* (2017) and the coeditor of *American Political Thought: An Alternative View* (2017).